FOURTH EDITION

Tennis

STEPS TO SUCCESS

Jim Brown
Camille Soulier

HUMAN KINETICS

Library of Congress Cataloging-in-Publication Data

Brown, Jim, 1940-
  Tennis : steps to success / Jim Brown, Camille Soulier. -- Fourth edition.
    pages cm
  1. Tennis. I. Title.
  GV995.B6924 2013
  796.342--dc23

                                          2012044147

ISBN-10: 1-4504-3208-5 (print)
ISBN-13: 978-1-4504-3208-5 (print)

The web addresses cited in this text were current as of February 2013, unless otherwise noted.

Acquisitions Editor: Justin Klug
Developmental Editor: Laura E. Podeschi
Assistant Editor: Tyler M. Wolpert
Copyeditor: Patsy Fortney
Graphic Designer: Keri Evans
Cover Designer: Keith Blomberg
Photograph (cover): Eyewire photodisc
Photographs (interior): Michael Marengo, unless otherwise noted
Photo Production Manager: Jason Allen
Art Manager: Kelly Hendren
Associate Art Manager: Alan L. Wilborn
Illustrations: © Human Kinetics
Printer: Versa Press

Human Kinetics books are available at special discounts for bulk purchase. Special editions or book excerpts can also be created to specification. For details, contact the Special Sales Manager at Human Kinetics.

Printed in the United States of America   10 9 8 7 6 5 4 3 2 1

The paper in this book is certified under a sustainable forestry program.

Human Kinetics
Website: www.HumanKinetics.com

United States: Human Kinetics
P.O. Box 5076
Champaign, IL 61825-5076
800-747-4457
e-mail: humank@hkusa.com

Canada: Human Kinetics
475 Devonshire Road Unit 100
Windsor, ON N8Y 2L5
800-465-7301 (in Canada only)
e-mail: info@hkcanada.com

Europe: Human Kinetics
107 Bradford Road
Stanningley
Leeds LS28 6AT, United Kingdom
+44 (0) 113 255 5665
e-mail: hk@hkeurope.com

Australia: Human Kinetics
57A Price Avenue
Lower Mitcham, South Australia 5062
08 8372 0999
e-mail: info@hkaustralia.com

New Zealand: Human Kinetics
P.O. Box 80
Torrens Park, South Australia 5062
0800 222 062
e-mail: info@hknewzealand.com

E5779

To the memory of Clyde and Martien Brown
and Milton G. and Leah St. Martin Soulier

Contents

Climbing the Steps to Tennis Success

The sport of tennis has changed—from the way a racket is constructed to the way it is held, the way it is swung, and the strategy used in singles and doubles.

Although tennis will continue to change, the fundamentals will not. The "anything goes" look of today's strokes is effective only if there has been a structured approach to learning the game that allows each player to find his or her unique style of play.

The fourth edition of *Tennis: Steps to Success* provides that approach for players, teachers, and coaches. With it, you can build a solid foundation or improve on the one you've already developed. Every paragraph, drill, illustration, and color photograph in this new edition has been reexamined, rewritten, or added by two authors who have played, taught, and coached the sport. There is something new on every page.

In steps 1 through 8, beginners can build their games with forehands, backhands, serves, and volleys before learning how to use specialty shots such as the half volley, lob, overhead smash, and drop shot. They can measure their success on a 10-point scale for each of the 84 drills in the book.

Intermediates can progress far beyond basic strokes, increasing and refining their skills with game- and match-specific drills as they move closer to becoming an advanced tennis player. Using steps 9 through 11, they can put their collection of strokes into a game plan that includes big-picture strategies and point-by-point tactics.

Instructors and teaching professionals who have established systems can select from the drills, activities, and grading systems to enhance their programs. The Sport of Tennis introduction includes a brief history of tennis, updated equipment details, and an explanation of rules. An appendix has been added that contains evidence-based guidelines for warming up and cooling down, plus an expanded discussion of common tennis injuries—how to recognize, treat, and hopefully prevent them. If you or your students are new to tennis, the glossary contains 189 terms.

Coaches continually add pieces of information to their personal tennis databases. *Tennis: Steps to Success* accelerates this process. In addition to the fundamentals of stroke production, more than 250 suggestions are included in the final three steps on singles tactics, doubles tactics, and special situations.

The success of this book and the entire *Steps to Success* series is based on a systematic but flexible approach to playing and teaching. Tennis players and teachers around the world follow the same sequence of learning activities as they work through each step. Previous editions of *Tennis: Steps to Success* have sold more than 100,000 copies in English and have been translated into seven languages.

With this book, you are assured of getting the following court-tested teaching and learning components:

Stroke Fundamentals   Steps 1 through 8 provide explanations for executing each stroke and images that give you a mental picture of how to hit the ball. The explanations include tips for getting into position, gripping the racket correctly, taking it back, swinging, and following through.

Color Photos   Color photos have replaced line drawings. Each step has multiple images of real tennis players demonstrating correct techniques.

Self-Paced Drills   The self-paced drills for each stroke are designed to be performed in the order in which they appear. You should keep score along the way. The drills are diagrammed and explained in terms that have been successfully used with thousands of students.

Levels of Difficulty   Following each drill are suggestions for making it more or less difficult, depending on the skill level of the player. Almost any drill can be made challenging for a beginning, an intermediate, or in some instances, an advanced player.

Success Checks   Every player needs key reminders about stroke production. Success checks are cues the player and the teacher can use to improve technique without overloading either of them with too much information.

Missteps and Corrections   There are no perfect tennis players. All of them make mistakes. Missteps tell you what to look for, and corrections explain how to fix the problem. Players who are familiar with common mistakes ahead of time may be able to avoid them altogether.

Success Summaries   Near the end of each step is a success summary—a quick review of what you've learned in that step.

Scoring Summaries   The scoring summary is a worksheet at the end of each step to record your scores. Almost every drill in the book is based on a 10-point scoring system. Perhaps you're almost a 10 on some strokes. If so, you're not a beginner anymore.

Your reward for completing *Tennis: Steps to Success* is up to you. You may simply want to enjoy a sport that provides a lifetime of healthy activity. Your goal might be to become a tournament-level player, or you may want to guide others as they discover the sport. Whoever you are, wherever you live and work, and whatever your goal, *Tennis: Steps to Success* is ready to help you become the best player, teacher, or coach you can be.

Acknowledgments

We would like to thank all of the people who helped make *Tennis: Steps to Success* possible, especially those in Hattiesburg, Mississippi. The book's photo sessions became a community effort involving the Hattiesburg City Recreation Department and the Racket Club of Hattiesburg (who allowed us to use their courts) and more than a dozen Hattiesburg residents.

Michael Marengo, our talented photographer, deserves special recognition. He spent countless hours taking more than 1,500 photos, communicating with Human Kinetics photographer Neil Bernstein, and helping us select the final 80-plus color photos that appear in the book.

The following Hattiesburg players volunteered to be photo models, ball shaggers, court sweepers, drivers, and production assistants:

Lilly Brady	Ethan Marengo
Jean Denton	Katherine Marengo
Debra Dobbins	Nicholas Marengo
Bronagh Gallagher	Brad Martin
Betty King	Todd Martin
Margo Lamunyon	Lauren Sanford
David Lawrence, Jr.	Nicholas Whitehead
Hannah Lee	Trey Williams
Barney Hebert	Melissa Graves

Finally, we want to express our appreciation to Human Kinetics and acquisitions editor Justin Klug, who gave us the opportunity to write the book, and Laura Podeschi, our developmental editor, who was helpful, professional, and pleasant throughout the process.

The Sport of Tennis

For a 41-year-old Welshman named Walter Clopton Wingfield, 1874 was a good year. The British army officer received a patent for a game he called sphairistike (alternately, lawn tennis); he published a 40-page rules book; and he sold more than a thousand kits that included a net, posts, balls, and rackets.

The popularity of the game spread quickly, but players and officials soon dropped the name *sphairistike* in favor of *lawn tennis* (and later, simply *tennis*), and they changed Wingfield's hourglass-shaped court to one that was longer and rectangular. Players also figured out that they didn't need Wingfield's kit to play the game, sales sagged, and he let the patent expire after three years.

AN EVOLVING GAME

Even though Major Wingfield had borrowed elements from similar games that had been played for hundreds (perhaps thousands) of years in various parts of the world, he is generally given credit for inventing the game of tennis as we know it. He didn't get rich with his invention, but he played an important role in the development of a sport in which others have made millions and became superstars. Wingfield's accomplishments led to his induction into the International Tennis Hall of Fame in Newport, Rhode Island, in 1997—85 years after his death.

It didn't take long for tennis to become an international sport. The first Wimbledon tournament was held in 1877; the first U.S. Open, in 1881; the first French Open, in 1891; and what would later be known as the Australian Open, in 1905. These four tournaments are now known as Grand Slam events.

Pioneers

Tennis had a history of being slow to include minorities, women, and people from middle and lower socioeconomic groups. For too long, it was a sport played mostly by wealthy men who belonged to exclusive clubs, but things started to change after World War II.

Richard "Pancho" Gonzales, a public-court, self-taught power player who won two U.S. Open titles (1948 and 1949) before turning pro at the age of 21, cracked the door for other great Hispanic-American players. Althea Gibson (11 Grand Slam titles in the late 1950s) and Arthur Ashe (5 Grand Slam titles from 1967 to 1977) opened the door for African-American players. And Billie Jean King, who won 6 Wimbledon championships and 4 U.S. Open titles from 1963 to 1975, knocked the doors down in her fight for women's pay and women's rights in the world of tennis and beyond.

These pioneers and others (see the sidebar, Game Changers) made it possible for the sport to be played by people of all classes and from all ethnic backgrounds almost everywhere in the world. Most of the 30 million players in the United States play on

GAME CHANGERS

Walter Wingfield gets credit for inventing the game we know as tennis, but many others did things on and off the court that changed the game in profound ways. Here are 11 of them, in no particular order, all of whom have been inducted into the International Tennis Hall of Fame.

Bill Tilden   Arguably the world's best and most visible player during the 1920s and early 1930s, Tilden won seven U.S. Championships and played on seven Davis Cup teams. He wrote tennis instruction books that were used for decades.

Jack Kramer   Kramer pioneered the attacking game and dominated amateur and professional tennis in the late 1940s and early 1950s. The Jack Kramer Autograph Wilson racket sold 10 million frames. Later, he was a promoter, a commentator, and the first director of the Association of Tennis Professionals (ATP).

Richard Gonzales   Largely self-taught, Gonzales overcame racism and discrimination to win back-to-back U.S. Open titles in 1948 and 1949. He elevated the serve-and-volley game to a new level and was a colorful, major force in professional tennis for two decades.

Althea Gibson   Gibson broke the color barrier when she played in the 1950 U.S. Championships. She won five Grand Slam events, including singles titles at Wimbledon in 1957 and 1958.

Harry Hopman   Coach Harry Hopman's Australian teams won the Davis Cup 16 times, and he may have been the greatest Davis Cup coach ever. He taught and coached many of the world's elite players in Australia and later in the United States.

Gladys Heldman   Heldman founded *World Tennis* magazine. She played a key role in creating and developing the Virginia Slims Circuit for women pros, the first separate circuit for women and the precursor to the Women's Tennis Association (WTA).

Bud Collins   Collins was internationally known as a tennis writer, journalist, and historian. Later, he became the voice and the face of televised tennis as a commentator. He has entertained and educated generations of tennis fans, and added to the popularity of the sport.

Lamar Hunt   Hunt was perhaps the most important promoter of professional tennis in the world. He created World Championship Tennis and, according to the International Tennis Hall of Fame, "changed the way the world looked at the game."

Billie Jean King   King won 10 Grand Slam events and has been called the most important female athlete of all time. She was the first president of the WTA and became the world's leading advocate of women's and team tennis.

Arthur Ashe   Ashe won titles in all four Grand Slam events. More than being a tennis champion, this African American was recognized throughout the world as a sportsman, statesman, activist, and ambassador for the sport of tennis.

Mark McCormack   McCormack's International Management Group became the largest firm in the world to represent athletes. He raised the profile of tennis with clients such as Billie Jean King, Chris Evert, Bjorn Borg, Pete Sampras, and Monica Seles.

public courts, and most are amateurs who play for fun with friends, in tournaments, on teams, or in leagues. About half of all U.S. players are women.

Open Tennis

Open tennis meant that, for the first time, professional players were able to compete in tournaments traditionally restricted to amateurs. Before open tennis, money was paid covertly to some of the world's best players, even though they retained their status as amateurs.

Players such as Jack Kramer, Pancho Gonzales, Pancho Segura, and Bobby Riggs barnstormed the United States, touring the country and playing short-duration events before small crowds in small venues. Some called it "the secret tennis tour."

Open tennis was not a universally popular concept. The International Tennis Federation (ITF), for example, threatened to prohibit players from entering its tournaments if they turned pro.

Businessmen and promoters such as Kramer, Lamar Hunt, Dave Dixon, and George MacCall had most of the world's best professional players under contract. They convinced (perhaps coerced) the tennis establishment to allow their contract professionals to play in Grand Slam and other high-profile tournaments. When tournament officials reluctantly agreed to let the pros in, the promoters threatened to keep those same players out until they were given substantial prize money.

The first "Open Era" tournament was held in Bournemouth, England, in 1968. The first open Grand Slam event was the French Open. Open Era tennis elevated the quality of play, increased the number of spectators at tournaments, and made the sport of tennis more attractive to television audiences.

Television

Television changed the game of tennis, mostly in good ways. In 1972, more than 50 million viewers watched Australian stars Ken Rosewall and Rod Laver play a five-set classic. Rosewall won. A year later, Billie Jean King defeated the once-great but aging tennis hustler Riggs in the Battle of the Sexes. The match took place in the Astrodome in Houston, Texas, before a crowd of 30,000. Millions more watched on TV. Superstar names boosted ratings. The Grand Slam tournaments began to attract viewers from other sports who were not hard-core players or fans.

The number of recreational players soared. Tennis-related products created an economic boom that appeared to be directly related to the number of tennis events shown on television. The tennis accessories that players wore and used, the synthetic surfaces on which they played, and even the sport drinks and energy bars they consumed had a crossover marketing effect on other sports seeking to benefit from bigger television audiences and lucrative sponsorships.

American stars Jimmy Connors and John McEnroe played brilliantly during the 1970s and 1980s in nationally televised matches. However, their frequent unruly behavior on the court (which included cursing, throwing rackets, and arguing with officials) set an example that may have negatively influenced a generation of young players.

Television even changed the way score is kept. With traditional scoring, the length of matches is unpredictable, making it more difficult to slot advertising and to manage a schedule. Therefore, tiebreaker games were introduced in some cases so a 6-6 set would end quickly.

Technology

Technology continues to change the sport of tennis. At one time courts were made of grass, clay, or concrete. Now they are made of synthetic materials with made-to-order surfaces that affect the pace of play. Slower courts result in longer points. Faster courts equal shorter points.

Rackets were traditionally made of wood, but in the 1970s racket construction evolved to include materials such as aluminum, graphite, boron, fiberglass, Kevlar, and carbon fiber. Today, composite rackets allow players to hit hard from any position on or behind the court, regardless of technique. Serve-and-volley tennis of the '70s, '80s, and '90s emphasized big serves, getting to the net early in a point, and finishing with a volley or overhead smash. That style has given way to serve-and-stay-back tennis, emphasizing big serves (some clock in at the 140 to 150 mph, or 225 to 241 km/h, range), powerful groundstrokes, and long rallies. Volleys are less important in singles because players don't want to risk being passed at the net by a technology-aided forehand or backhand.

Technology changed the size of racket heads from 60 to 70 square inches (387 to 451 sq cm) to jumbo-sized models. Racket heads are now between 95 and 118 square inches (613 to 761 sq cm). Racket head thickness changed from narrow to wide and back to narrow again.

Instruction

Finally, tennis instruction and coaching are more available today than ever before. Tennis pros, teachers, coaches, camps, courses, recreation department programs, and clinics are easily accessible. Tennis organizations and companies conduct training schools and certification programs at many levels to produce future teaching professionals.

The availability of information regarding every facet of the game has, for the most part, elevated the level of play. Unfortunately, Internet information is scattered and sometimes inaccurate. It often raises more questions than it provides helpful answers. The following section on equipment will answer some of those questions.

EQUIPMENT

Beginner, intermediate, and advanced players all have decisions to make regarding rackets, balls, shoes, and apparel. This section provides some suggestions for buying, using, and taking care of these products.

Rackets

Babolat, Donnay, Dunlop, Head, Prince, ProKennex, Slazenger, Volkl, Wilson, and Yonex are some of the brand names that you are likely to see. Labels, cards, stickers, and hangtags on the rackets provide valuable information about racket size, length, string tension, flexibility, and other features.

Approximately 75 percent of all tennis rackets are factory prestrung. Rackets for beginners are made of aluminum or low-end graphite, and they sell for between $30 and $90 (USD).

The other 25 percent of rackets are priced between $90 and $400 and are made of materials such as composite graphite, carbon fiber, and Kevlar. Intermediate players typically upgrade to an unstrung racket in the $100 to $165 range.

RACKET RECOMMENDATIONS FOR BEGINNERS

Length: 27 inches (686 mm)
Grip size: 4 1/4 to 4 1/2 inches (108 to 114 mm)
Racket head size: 100 to 110 square inches (645 to 710 sq cm)
Weight: 8.5 to 10 ounces (241 to 283 g)
Construction materials: Aluminum or graphite
Strings: Prestrung nylon, synthetic gut
Price: $30 to $90

Be careful. Rackets that look alike, have roughly the same features, and cost about the same can play completely differently, depending on the player. What works for one player is not necessarily comfortable for another. Experiment with many rackets before spending a lot of money. Using dealer demos is a good idea.

In the late 1980s, rackets weighed between 11 and 14 ounces (312 and 397 g). By 1995, minimum racket weight had dropped to 9 ounces (255 g). Ten years later, you could find rackets as light as 8 ounces (227 g) and as heavy as 12.5 ounces (354 g). More recently, a survey of more than 200 racket models found the lightest at 8.3 ounces (235 g) and the heaviest at 11.8 ounces (335 g).

Beginners—both males and females—should look for rackets that are on the light-weight end of the range and that are relatively stiff. Lighter rackets should have the weight distributed toward the racket head to generate racket speed—more power. Heavier rackets require the effort and skill usually associated with intermediate or advanced players.

Generally, stiffer rackets provide more control, allowing for a harder swing or the player rebounding a faster ball by using a short backswing. Flexible rackets provide more power and less directional control, but both can be altered by adjusting string tension, the length of the swing, and the velocity of the swing.

Regardless of flexibility, controlling the ball is more a function of the player's skill than the type of racket. There is no universal measure of racket flexibility, and each company has its own method of describing that feature. Read all you can about a racket's flexibility (and other features) and talk to a salesperson who knows something about racket construction. You are more likely to find that person at a tennis specialty or pro shop than at a sporting goods or other retail store.

The ability to understand or ask questions about the various parts of a racket will help you make the right decision in buying one. Figure 1 illustrates everything from the butt of the racket to the tip.

As you progress along the *Steps to Success*, you will develop your own swing style. For example, if you have a short backswing (how far you take the racket back when preparing to hit a shot), you'll probably do better with a stiff racket. Players with longer backswings usually prefer flexible rackets. Some have an intermediate-length backswing and should look for a racket with moderate flexibility.

Each racket company has its own method of matching swing style with the right racket. Look for the information on the racket, attached to it, or on the product's website. Beginning players don't have to worry about swing style. They won't know what their style is until they begin taking lessons or playing.

Although rackets are lighter today, racket heads may be bigger than in the past. Head sizes range from 95 to 118 square inches (613 to 761 sq cm), and most recreational

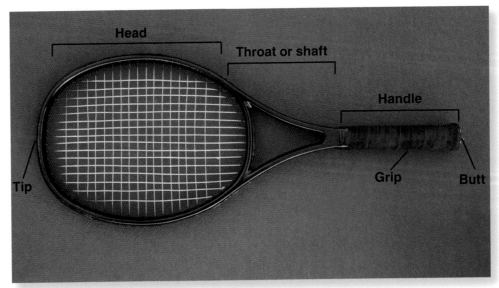

Figure 1 Parts of a tennis racket.

players do best with bigger heads, although not necessarily the biggest, because they give players a larger surface with which to make contact.

Grip sizes have been consistent over the past few decades. Each racket model comes in these sizes: 4, 4 1/8, 4 1/4, 4 3/8, 4 1/2, and 4 5/8 inches (10, 10.48, 10.80, 11.11, 11.43, and 11.75 cm). The most common sizes are 4 3/8 and 4 1/2 inches (11.11 and 11.43 cm). Look for the grip size information on the side of the handle, just above the grip or on the butt cap.

DETERMINING GRIP SIZE

Here are five ways—all of them time tested, but none of them particularly scientific—to determine the correct grip size for your hand.

1. Shake hands with the racket (which will provide you with an Eastern forehand grip, as explained in step 1). As your fingers curl around the grip, the end of your thumb should touch the first joint of your middle finger (figure 2).

Figure 2 The end of the thumb meets the first joint of the middle finger.

2. Measure the distance from the long crease in the middle of your palm (the second line down from the base of your fingers) to the tip of your ring finger. Position a ruler between your ring and middle fingers. The distance measured should be very close to the correct racket circumference grip for your hands (figure 3).

3. Hold the racket in your dominant hand. It should feel comfortable and easy to maneuver. The shape of the grip should fit the contour of your hand.

4. Hold the racket in an Eastern forehand grip (see step 1). You should be able to fit the index finger of your non-hitting hand in the space between your ring finger and palm (figure 4). If there isn't enough room for your index finger, the grip is too small. If there is space between your finger and palm, the grip is too big.

5. Play with a demo or loaner racket. If it twists in your hand on contact, the grip might be too small. If your hand and arm quickly tire, it might be too big.

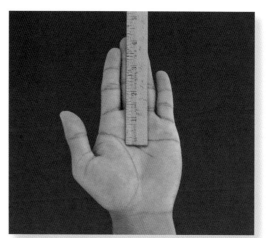

Figure 3   Measure from the tip of your ring finger to the second line in your palm.

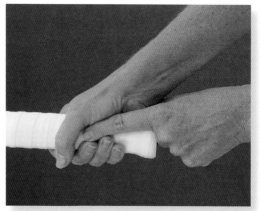

Figure 4   Fit the index finger of your nonhitting hand in the space between your palm and ring finger.

STRINGS

Performance rackets—those that cost more and are used by intermediate and advanced players—are sold unstrung. The majority of players use strings made of nylon or other synthetic materials, such as polyester or Kevlar. The few who use strings made of gut (beef intestines) are either very good players or very serious about their games.

Table 1 String Characteristics

String type	Advantages	Disadvantages
Gut	Better feel, or touch	Higher cost, less durable
Synthetic gut	Lower cost, more durable	Slightly less feel, or touch
Nylon	Lowest cost, durable	Less resilient
String gauge	**Advantages**	**Disadvantages**
Thicker (15 gauge)	More durable	Less feel, or touch
Thinner (16-17 gauge)	Better feel, or touch	Less durable
String tension	**Advantages**	**Disadvantages**
Lower tension	More power	Less control
Higher tension	More control	Less power

Expect to pay $15 to $18 for nylon strings, $18 to $28 for synthetic gut strings, and $45 to $65 for a racket strung with gut strings. Again, look for a suggested string tension label on the racket throat.

String tension ranges from 55 to 74 pounds (25 to 34 kg). Generally, the lower the tension, the more power that can be generated. Tighter strings allow for more control, assuming you are a good enough player to control the ball regardless of racket flexibility and string tension. Settle on a string tension that gives you the best combination of power and control, which is usually 4 to 5 pounds (1.8 to 2.3 kg) from the top of the range (see table 1).

Beginners don't usually break strings. They just play with rackets until the strings lose enough tension to affect power or control. How often should a racket be restrung? Approximately as many times a year as you play during a week. For example, if you are a moderate hitter and you play twice a week, get your racket strung twice a year.

TAKING CARE OF RACKETS AND STRINGS

Rackets endure a lot of abuse during the course of a lesson, practice session, or match. Make them last longer and stay stronger by following these suggestions:

- Avoid storing rackets in hot, cold, or damp places.
- Keep racket covers on rackets when they are not being used.
- Don't spin the racket on the court to determine serve and side.
- Don't use the racket to pick up balls if the frame scrapes the court.
- Wipe the strings clean after playing on a damp court or in high humidity.
- Use a replacement grip or overwrap when the original grip tears or becomes slick.

- Don't toss your racket, bounce it off the court, or hit things other than the ball with it.

- Check your racket for warping and cracks before getting it restrung.

- If a string breaks, remove all the strings to relieve tension on the frame.

The more often intermediate and advanced players play, the more often their strings break. What should you do when strings break too often? Following are a few suggestions. Also, ask a racket stringing professional for advice.

- Use a thicker gauge of the same string.

- Try a more durable construction of the same material in the strings that have been breaking.

- Try a different type or gauge of synthetic strings.

- Use a racket that has a denser string pattern.

Tennis Balls

A can of three premium quality balls costs $2.50 to $8.00 at some specialty or pro shops. A mass merchandiser or sporting goods store sells them for less. Three dollars is an average price.

Save a little more by buying a packet of three or four cans of tennis balls. Typical prices are $15 for six cans and $20 for eight cans—or about $2.50 per can. Teachers and coaches sometimes buy used tennis balls from club professionals after tournaments.

Even if you are a beginner, buy the best tennis balls available. Wilson and Penn are two of the more prominent companies that make quality tennis balls. Look for information on the container indicating that the balls are used for "Championship Play" and have been approved by the United States Tennis Association or the International Tennis Federation.

Most balls are packaged in clear plastic containers under pressure. If the pressure has not been maintained and the balls are soft when the can is opened, return it to the dealer for a refund or a new can.

Three balls may last two or three outings for beginners and some intermediates, but after that they will begin to lose their pressure and bounce, or the felt will begin to wear off. When that happens, use them for practice only. Extend the life of balls by keeping them in the original container and by storing them in a cool place.

Ask for extra-duty balls if you are going to play on hard surfaces. Regular (championship) balls are used on softer surfaces because they don't wear as quickly. Tennis balls sold for play in high altitudes should be designated as high-altitude balls. Don't take heavy-duty or championship balls with you on a vacation to a high-altitude city. Buy them when you get there.

Shoes

Discount stores sell varieties of affordable shoes that will get you through a tennis course or a series of lessons. However, if you plan to play tennis three or more times a week, you should wear a sport-specific court shoe.

Look for soft, flexible soles if you are going to be playing and practicing on soft, claylike courts. Even serious players can get months out of a pair of shoes on soft surfaces. Wear tennis shoes with soles that are flexible and have added tread if you

SHOE-TAP TEST

Buying new tennis shoes? First, take the shoe-tap test.

1. Put on and lace up new shoes.

2. Tap the heels of your feet down into the heels of the shoes.

3. Stand up without wiggling your feet into position to fit the shoe arches.

4. If the arch is in the proper position without maneuvering your foot, the shoe fits.

are going to play on hard courts. Don't be surprised if your shoes wear out within a few weeks.

Perhaps the most important feature of true tennis shoes is lateral control—inside and outside stability. Tennis players spend more time moving from side to side along the baseline than they do going forward and backward. That means you'll need a shoe sole that is not as steep on the sides (from the sole to the ground) as a cross-trainer or running shoe.

Other factors to consider are weight (buy the lightest shoe possible if other features meet your needs), comfort (walk, run, and change directions during the in-store test period), and cost (appearance and brand are not necessarily consistent with quality construction).

Socks

Tennis shoes get most of the publicity, but serious players know that the socks inside those shoes can affect performance and prevent injuries. Socks designed specifically for tennis players are thick or double-layered, with extra padding for the toe and heel. Some socks are so thick and cushioned that you might have to buy shoes a half-size larger than usual. The materials to look for in tennis socks, in the order of how well they repel sweat and expose it to air for quick evaporation, are Coolmax, acrylic, polypropylene, and wool. Remember: No cotton socks for tennis. Not only are they poor in wicking moisture away from the foot, but they also lose their shape, bunch up, and quickly become abrasive.

Apparel

The good news is that you can find moderately priced, high-quality tennis outfits at sporting goods, department, and discount stores, and at some pro and specialty shops. The bad news is that you can spend a lot of money on trendy shirts, shorts, skirts, warm-ups, and other active-wear clothing.

Students in high school and college activity classes usually wear shorts and shirts approved by the school, but not necessarily old-style physical education uniforms. There may be dress codes, but no emphasis is put on fashion. If you take private or group lessons or compete in tennis events, there are usually guidelines to follow. A few facilities still require all-white attire; those indications will be in the entry information. Refrain from wearing muscle shirts, tank tops, and swimsuits. Use common sense, observe what others are wearing, and ask someone in charge what kind of dress is appropriate.

Most serious players practice in the most comfortable clothes they can find—T-shirts and baggy shorts are okay. They play matches in the best-looking outfits they can afford. Wearing loose-fitting clothes for comfortable movement and light-colored outfits for coolness is more important than dressing for style. In hot-weather months, consider wearing a hat. It will keep the perspiration from running down your face and give a little protection against harmful sun rays.

PLAYING A GAME, SET, AND MATCH

Singles is a match between two players. Doubles is a match among four players—two on each team. Mixed doubles is a match pairing a man and woman on one team against a man and woman on the other team. One-up, one-down wheelchair tennis pairs a wheelchair player with an able-bodied player competing against a team also composed of a wheelchair player and an able-bodied player.

After a 10-minute warm-up, the players decide by spinning a racket or flipping a coin who will serve first and on which end of the court they will begin the match (for more details, see Singles Rules). The server has two chances to put the ball in play, and the point is played out. After the serve, players may hit the ball before or after it bounces once on the court. Points are won when the opponent hits into the net or outside the boundary lines.

One player serves an entire game, which may last from 4 points to an infinite number of points. The first point of every game always begins on the right side of the baseline. The server alternates serving the first point from the right side of the baseline and the second point from the left side. The receiver also moves back and forth from right to left to return the serve (in singles; for information specific to doubles, see Doubles Rules).

A set is won when one player has won at least 6 games and is ahead by at least 2 games. The final score in a set would be 6-0, 6-1, 6-2, 6-3, 6-4, 7-5, 8-6, and so on. Note that this win-by-two rule varies depending on the level of play; in many cases, tiebreakers are used instead. For more specific information regarding scoring, see the Scoring section.

A recreational player wins a match by winning 2 out of 3 sets. Male professionals must win 3 out of 5 sets in a few big tournaments and 2 out of 3 in most other events, whereas female professionals must win 2 out of 3 sets in all tournaments. When time is limited, pro sets might constitute a match. An 8-game pro set is won by the player who wins at least 8 games and who is ahead by at least 2 games. Players change ends of the court when the total number of games played at any time during a set is an odd number.

In most matches, players are responsible for keeping their own scores and for calling their opponents' shots out of bounds. No sound from a player means the ball is in, and play continues. Balls that hit the lines are in play. Shouting "out" means the ball landed outside the boundary line and the point is over.

In some tournament competitions, an umpire may stand or sit near the net, call out the score, and settle disputes on close shots. At higher levels of the game, linespersons are positioned to make line calls. Figure 5*a* illustrates the lines and areas of the court; figure 5*b*, court dimensions.

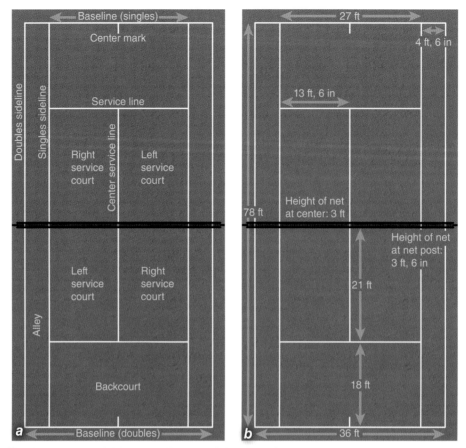

Figure 5 Tennis court *(a)* lines and areas; *(b)* dimensions.

A match may also refer to competition between two teams representing schools, clubs, or other groups. Within each match, points make up games, games make up sets, and sets make up matches.

A tennis tournament involves teams or individuals competing against other teams or individuals in a series of matches. A high school or college team, for example, may enter a single-elimination tournament. With one loss a team is eliminated from championship competition (although in some cases may move into a consolation bracket). The U.S. Open and Wimbledon are examples of single-elimination tournaments for the best players in the world. In a double-elimination tournament, which is rarely used in tennis, an individual or team that loses two matches is out. A round-robin tournament involves an individual or team competing against all of the other players or teams entered in that tournament. The team with the best overall win–loss record wins the tournament. In the case of a tie, head-to-head match results may be used.

Singles Rules

Players take all practice shots before the match begins. Warm-ups are usually limited to 10 minutes. The player who wins the racket spin or coin toss may choose to serve or to receive, or on which side of the court to play the first game. The winner also has the option to relinquish the first choice to the opponent. The other player gets to choose whatever the winner hasn't chosen—serve or receive, or side of court. Read step 9, Singles Tactics, for tactical considerations regarding these options.

To begin a game, the server stands behind the baseline to the right of the center mark and inside the singles sideline, facing the net (figure 6). When the opponent is ready, the server has two chances to put the ball into play by tossing it into the air and hitting it into the service court across the net and diagonally opposite from the baseline serving position. The server cannot step on or beyond the baseline before striking the ball.

If the receiver makes any attempt to return the serve, she is indicating that she is ready to begin play. The receiver can stand anywhere, but must let the serve bounce before returning it. After each point, the server alternates between the left and right sides of the center mark to serve. If a served ball hits the top of the net and goes into the proper court, "let" is called and the serve is replayed.

Players win a point if the opponent does any of the following:

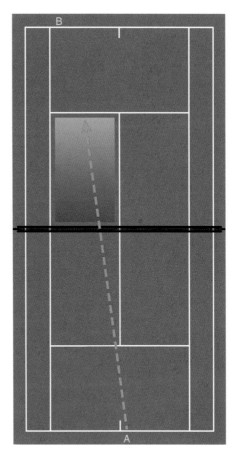

Figure 6   Player positioning when beginning a singles game.

- Fails in both attempts to serve the ball into the proper court

- Hits the ball outside the proper boundary lines

- Hits the ball into the net

- Lets the ball bounce twice before returning it

- Reaches over the net to hit a ball before it has bounced

- Throws the racket and hits the ball

- Touches the net with her body or racket while the ball is in play

- Deliberately carries or catches the ball on the racket strings

- Does anything to hinder the opponent in making a shot

- Touches the ball with anything other than the racket during play

- Touches or catches the ball during play, even if standing outside the court

Doubles Rules

The server may stand anywhere behind the baseline between the center mark and the doubles sideline (figure 7). The four players take turns serving an entire game. The order of serving stays the same throughout the set. In a game of AC versus BD, A serves, then B or D serves, then C, then B or D (whoever did not serve the second game). Receivers choose the right or left side to receive serve throughout the set. Other rules described for singles apply to doubles, except that after the serve, the alleys between the singles and doubles sidelines are in play. Only one player on a doubles team can strike the ball before it goes over the net.

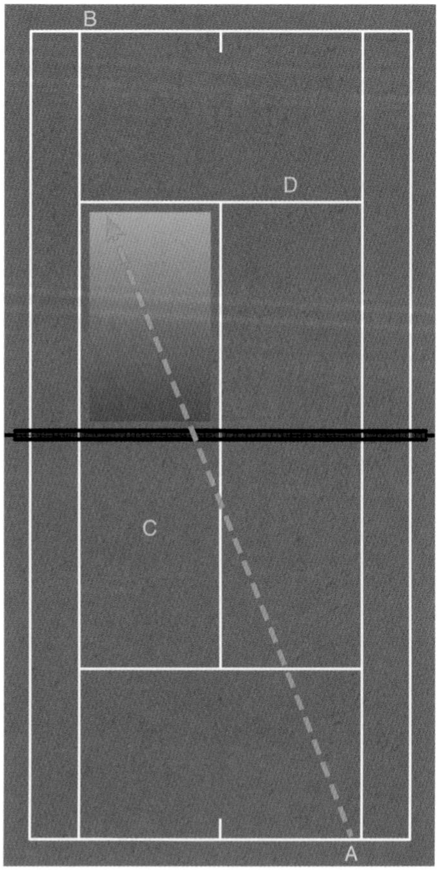

Scoring

The server's score is always called out first. Points are called love (0), 15 (the first point won by either player), 30 (the second point), 40 (the third point), and game (the fourth point). If the players are tied at 3 or more points during a game, the score is called "deuce."

After deuce, if the server goes ahead by 1 point, the score is *ad in* or *advantage server*. If the receiver scores a point, it's *ad out*. A player must win 2 consecutive points after deuce to win the game. If not, the score is deuce again without limits to how many times it occurs.

Figure 7 Player positioning when beginning a doubles game.

NO-AD SCORING

No-ad scoring was introduced to simplify the method of keeping score and to reduce the time of matches. It is much easier for fans and players to learn and remember a simple 1-2-3 system than the 15-30-40-deuce-ad method.

Here is how no-ad scoring works:

- The first player to win 4 points wins the game.
- Points are 1, 2, 3, and game.
- When the score is tied at 3-3, the next point ends that game.
- At 3-3, the receiver chooses to receive the serve from either the right or left receiving court.

Because no-ad scoring eliminates the requirement of having to win games by at least 2 points, the overall length of tennis matches can be reduced considerably. Some high school and college matches are played on unlighted courts after school, before dark. No-ad scoring allows matches to be completed during daylight hours. Also, tournaments with large numbers of players, a restricted amount of time, and limited court space frequently use this method of scorekeeping. Matches are more likely to last between one hour and one hour, 15 minutes.

The disadvantage of no-ad scoring is that the well-conditioned athlete is penalized. The player who depends on endurance can use longer games and sets to wear down an opponent. Because no game will last more than 7 points, it may be possible for a player who gets a good start to gain an edge that cannot be overcome in a short match.

TIEBREAKERS

As mentioned earlier, tiebreakers were introduced so a 6-6 set could end more quickly than a regular set. Tiebreakers are scored as follows.

12-Point Tiebreaker   In a 12-point tiebreaker, the player or team that wins 7 points and is ahead by at least 2 points wins the tiebreaker and, therefore, a set. The score is called out as 1, 2, 3, 4, and so on throughout the game. A final tiebreaker score might be 7-0, 7-1, 7-2, 7-3, 7-4, 7-5, 8-6, 9-7, and so on (in points played). The set score would then be 7-6 or 6-7.

The singles player (or the player on the doubles team) whose turn it is to serve, serves the first point of the tiebreaker. The first server serves the first point from the right side of the court. The opponent then serves the second and third points, and after that, players serve alternately for 2 consecutive points until the winner of the tiebreak game and set has been decided. The second server serves the second and third points from the left and right courts, respectively, and this alternating-service system continues until the tiebreak game is completed.

Players change ends of the court after every 6 points and at the end of the tiebreaker. The player or team that served first in the tiebreak game receives in the first game of the next set.

Coman Tiebreaker   The Coman tiebreak procedure, according to the USTA, is the same 12-point tiebreaker, except that the players change ends after the first point, then after every 4 points (after the 5th, 9th, 13th, 17th points, and so on), and at the end of the tiebreaker (before the next set begins). The scoring is the same as a traditional tiebreaker, and the procedure is the same as a set or match tiebreaker. If the set score is 6-6, the player whose turn it is to serve serves the first point from the deuce court. After the first point, the players change ends and the following 2 points are served by the opponent in singles or opponents in doubles—that is, the player of the opposing team due to serve next—starting on the left side. Then each player or team serves alternately for 2 consecutive points (starting with the left side, or ad court). The opponents change ends after every 4 points until the end of the tiebreaker.

The Coman tiebreaker has two advantages:

1. The more frequent changing of ends results in elements such as the sun and wind being distributed more fairly between the two opponents. In the traditional 12-point tiebreaker, a player or team plays 6 consecutive points from the same end before changing sides.

2. In doubles, the server will always serve from the same end of the court that he did throughout the set, rather than having to serve from both ends.

COMAN TIEBREAKER HIGHLIGHTS

Following are some key ways the Coman tiebreaker differs from the 12-point tiebreaker:

- Players or teams change ends after the first point.
- Players or teams change ends every 4 points thereafter.
- In doubles, each player serves from the end of the court that was determined at the beginning of the set.

Super Tiebreaker A tiebreaker that is played in lieu of the third set is called a super tiebreaker, or 10-point tiebreaker. The super tiebreaker is played following either the 12-point or Coman tiebreaker procedures, except that the tiebreaker is played to 10; the first player or team to win 10 points when ahead by 2 wins the tiebreaker. The super tiebreaker is used in USTA league play, in many other USTA events, and at a growing number of high schools.

Unwritten Rules

Because most tennis matches are played on the honor system without officials, a few unwritten rules exist for players and spectators.

- If you ask someone to play a match, tennis balls are your responsibility.
- Take all practice serves before the first game begins, and not when it is your turn to serve the first time.
- In unofficiated matches, keep your own score. The server should announce the score prior to each point.
- Each player is responsible for calling balls out on her side of the court. If you are in doubt, the shot is good.
- Don't involve spectators in line calling. They are not in a position to make a call.
- Immediately and loudly make "out" calls. Never make calls on shots that are "in" during the rally.
- Disagreements of any kind between opponents should be resolved at the net in a quiet manner so others are not disturbed. If the point is not resolved, ask for an official, a tournament director, or the coach in charge, if available.
- If a loose ball on or behind the court interferes with concentration or becomes a safety hazard, call a let immediately and replay the point.
- If there is an unusual, uncontrolled delay between the first and second serves, allow your opponent to start the serving sequence over.
- Don't shout or distract your opponent in any way during a point.

- Don't groan, complain, curse, or verbally abuse yourself or others during a match.

- Avoid walking behind other courts during a point in progress.

- When returning a stray ball to its court, wait until the point has been completed on that court. Immediately returning the ball interferes with play.

- If one of your tennis balls rolls onto an adjacent court, wait for play on that court to stop before asking for your ball to be returned. "Thanks, court two," is one polite way to ask for help.

- Shake hands with your opponent at the net after a match.

- If you are a spectator, hold your applause or cheers until a point has been completed. Tennis players react to sound (as in "out" or "fault") and may stop a point if your noise is interpreted as a line call.

- Applaud or cheer well-played points, winning shots, and forced errors rather than unforced errors.

Key to Diagrams

———————➔ Running path

- - - - - - ➔ Path of tennis ball

A Player A

B Player B

C Player C

D Player D

F Feeder

S Server

R Receiver

SP Server's partner

RP Receiver's partner

Target area

Box

Forehands: Controlling the Rally

Tennis is about control—controlling the way you move on the court, controlling your swing, controlling your emotions, and controlling your opponent during points or rallies. And the first shot on your rally-control list is the forehand. It's the most frequently hit shot, the most natural, and the easiest to learn.

HITTING A FOREHAND

Think of the forehand as the foundation of your game. Build a strong base with your forehand, and it will support all of the other strokes. It can keep the point going until you are in a position to win it. Use it to move your opponent around the court and to take charge of a point. Your forehand can demoralize an opponent with its consistency, and if it's strong enough, the forehand can be your finisher—your closer.

You can even use a forehand to hide your weaknesses in other strokes. Is your backhand a problem? Position yourself on the court to hit more forehands. Still working on your serve? Compensate with a big forehand. Not very good at the net (yet)? Stay in the backcourt and pound the ball with forehands.

A good forehand tells your opponent that your forehand is a dangerous place to go. Steps 9 and 10 cover specific tactics for using the forehand in singles and doubles.

The forehand can be struck with a variety of racket angles, similar to the various pitches of golf club heads. Several options are available so that you can you can find a comfort zone and assume some of the responsibility for your playing style. Although most players have a basic forehand grip, they make slight changes in the grip during a point without realizing or remembering.

Every stroke in tennis consists of separate movements—preparation, swing, and follow-through. The goal is to make all of these movements come together in one smooth, efficient motion. The forehand starts with the feet, and good tennis players have good footwork. By getting to the right place on the court and positioning your feet in a way that works for you, you're setting the stage for a sequence of movements that concludes with a successful shot.

As your feet move to establish a hitting position, your hips and trunk get ready to transfer all that energy to your arm and racket. As you move the bottom half of your body into position, take the racket back approximately 180 degrees from your intended direction—far enough to generate some power when it's time to hit. In other words, as you set up for the forehand, your whole body is winding up. Sometimes you'll take a big windup; at other times you can make it short and compact. This sequence of events peaks when you swing to strike the ball, and it finishes with the follow-through (figure 1.1). Starting now, everything you learn about the forehand should eventually help you hit with power, control, and confidence.

Figure 1.1 FOREHAND

Preparation

1. Quick crossover or shuffle step to get to the ball
2. Eastern or semi-Western grip
3. Shoulder turn and racket back early
4. Square or semiopen stance

Swing

1. Upward and forward motion
2. Low-to-high swing path (waistline to shoulder height)
3. Early contact (out in front)

Follow-Through

1. Through the ball (fingernails point forward toward the net)
2. Up, out toward the net, and across (for the Eastern grip)
3. Up and across (for the semi-Western or Western grip)

MISSTEP

Your swing is inconsistent.

CORRECTION

Keep your wrist in a fixed, laid-back position. The more movement there is, the less control you have.

MISSTEP

You rush the swing or swing too late.

CORRECTION

Prepare to return a ball as soon as it leaves your opponent's racket, while it clears the net, or before it bounces on your side and comes toward you.

Players use four different forehand grips (Continental, Eastern, semi-Western, and Western); use four different stances (open, semiopen, closed, and square); and hit the ball with topspin, sidespin, underspin, or no spin. And we haven't even talked about backswings, swing paths, hitting zones, and follow-throughs.

Don't worry. Although all of these options are illustrated and discussed, certain grips, stances, and swings are recommended. Players can and have reached the elite level using such recommendations. Others discover the grips, stances, and follow-throughs that are effective for their particular body types and athletic ability, and they also reach the highest levels of the game. But beginners have to start somewhere. Forehand variations can be added or incorporated into your game as it matures.

Grips

Regardless of how you grip the racket with your dominant hand for a forehand, what you do with the other stays the same. Use your nondominant (off) hand to support the racket while making slight adjustments with your right hand if you are right-handed and left hand if left-handed. Using the off hand to adjust your grip has to become an automatic response. One-handed grip changes are not efficient.

Although we cover the Continental and Western grips in this section, the Eastern and semi-Western grips are recommend for the forehand.

EASTERN FOREHAND GRIP

With your nondominant hand, hold the racket at the throat, on edge, perpendicular to the court. With the other hand, shake hands with the racket so that your palm fits against the back bevel of the handle. This is the Eastern forehand grip (figure 1.2). Curl your fingers around the grip near its base. For a right-handed player who is holding the racket out to the right side, the wrist should be slightly to the right of the top, and the V formed by the thumb and index finger should be above but slightly toward the back part of the handle. A left-handed player should hold the racket so the wrist is slightly to the left of the top of the grip when looking down over the top.

The Eastern grip was once the most traditional way to hold the racket for a forehand, but it is no longer used by many of the top players. A problem occurs when teachers instruct their students to grip a racket the way elite players do, whether or not that grip is appropriate for less-than-elite players, because this is usually too

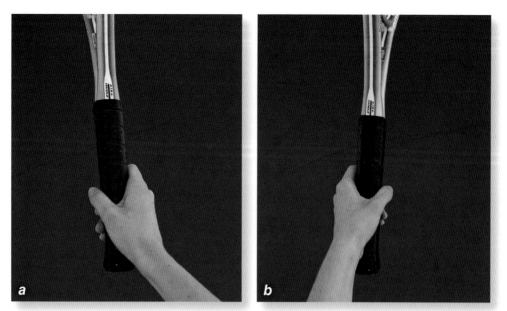

Figure 1.2 Eastern forehand grip: *(a)* for a right-handed player; *(b)* for a left-handed player.

much information for the students to absorb. A majority of teaching professionals stay with the Eastern forehand for beginners, but they allow their students to experiment with other grips as they become physically stronger and more advanced.

The advantages of the Eastern forehand are the natural position of the wrist, more reliance on the shoulder joint, less stress on the elbow and wrist, and an easier transition to net play. All are compelling arguments for using this grip. The disadvantages include not being able to hit with maximum power on some shots, not being able to hit topspin as effectively as with two other grips, and not being able to easily handle high-bouncing shots.

The Eastern forehand grip is a reasonable, practical choice for beginning, intermediate, and advanced players, but it won't receive a lot of support from teachers who work only with very good players. For them, the semi-Western is the first choice for the forehand.

SEMI-WESTERN GRIP

Hold the racket with the Eastern forehand grip. Now rotate your wrist to a position even farther behind the side of the grip. Think of it as being halfway between an Eastern and a Western grip (the Western grip is discussed in the next section). With the semi-Western grip (figure 1.3), you can hit the ball harder than with the Eastern grip, and it's easier to hit a ball with topspin. You can also strike the ball earlier and catch it on the rise.

The semi-Western grip has disadvantages. It may be harder for some beginners to master. It definitely is not a great grip for returning low-bouncing balls, and it's an inefficient grip for net play. It's also a more difficult adjustment to go from a semi-Western grip to one that can be used at the net on volleys. The switch from an Eastern forehand to a volleying grip is a smoother transition. Many players who use the semi-Western grip are never able to make the adjustments needed to volley and end up staying on the baseline indefinitely. If this grip is too uncomfortable, rotate your hand slightly back toward an Eastern grip. All of that said, the use of the semi-Western grip makes sense for a lot of very good players. Some start with the grip, and others grow into it.

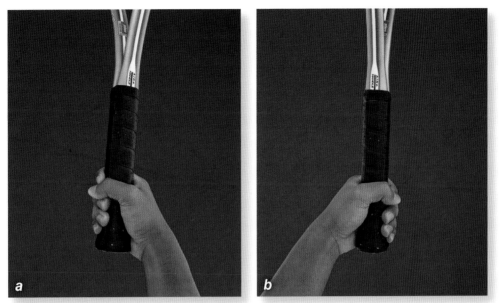

Figure 1.3   Semi-Western grip: *(a)* for a right-handed player; *(b)* for a left-handed player.

WESTERN GRIP

Again, start with the Eastern grip, wrist slightly to the right. Move it more to the right until you have the semi-Western. Okay, advance it one more turn until your palm is actually under the racket handle (figure 1.4). Feel weird? It looks weird, too, but some players learn to play with the Western forehand grip and are very successful with it.

The Western grip is especially popular with players who stay on the baseline and hit from an open stance. It's great for hitting with topspin and for taking high-bouncing balls, but that's about all. Hitting low-bouncing balls and balls that go wide to the forehand side is difficult using the Western grip. Western-grip players have a difficult time adapting to conventional grips for the volley.

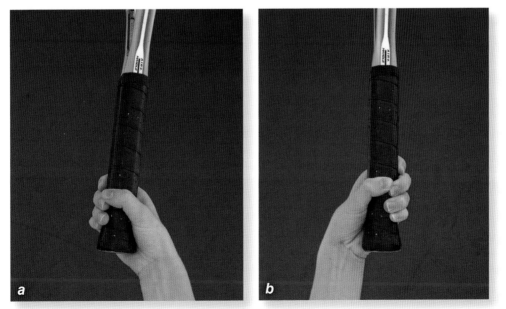

Figure 1.4   Western grip: *(a)* for a right-handed player; *(b)* for a left-handed player.

Unless you have a compelling reason to use the Western grip, don't. There may be occasions during a point when shifting to a Western grip will help you hit the ball with extreme topspin or allow you to hit one that bounces very high. Other than these occasions, you're better off with an Eastern grip or a semi-Western grip.

CONTINENTAL GRIP

There's one more grip to be discussed—the Continental grip. As with the Eastern grip, start by holding the racket perpendicular to the court and shaking hands so that your palm fits against the back of the handle. Instead of rotating your wrist to the right (for a right-handed player), move it a fraction of a turn to the left so that your wrist is directly on top of the racket handle. Extend your thumb along the grip so that the inside part is in contact with the flat bevel. If you are a left-handed player, move your wrist from left to right out of the Eastern forehand until your wrist is aligned on top. This position is the Continental grip (figure 1.5).

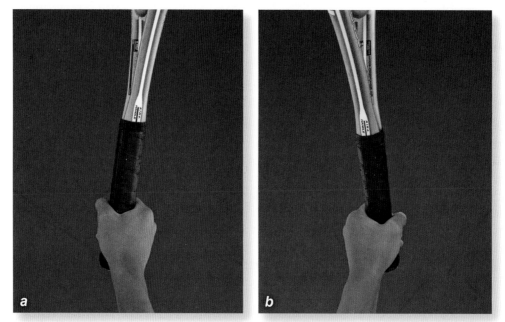

Figure 1.5 Continental grip: *(a)* for a right-handed player; *(b)* for a left-handed player.

Got all that? Don't use it, at least not for forehand groundstrokes. There are better and more comfortable ways to grip the racket for this shot. However, knowing how to hold a Continental grip will be useful when you reach step 3 (serves) and step 4 (volleys).

Whichever grip you decide to use, there are several simple activities that require only you, the racket, and one tennis ball. The simplest one is to dribble the ball on the court using the racket strings while holding the racket with the Eastern or semi-Western grip. It's something you'll do without even thinking about it for the rest of your tennis life, so you might as well get used to it now. To make things more interesting, dribble along any line on the court or turn your racket palm up and bounce the ball up instead of down. If you can do 100 up or down dribbles without a miss, you've got it. Move on to something else.

Ready Position

The one thing that hasn't changed about the forehand when changing grips is the ready position. It's the position in which you stand while anticipating your opponent's next shot. When you assume the ready position, it indicates that you are alert, poised for action, and watching the ball leave your opponent's racket.

In the ready position, your feet should be square to the net as you face it (figure 1.6). Hold the racket with a forehand grip unless you expect the ball to go somewhere else. Flex your knees slightly and lean with your weight forward on the balls of your feet. Place your hands and racket in front of your body, toward the net, as you extend your arms slightly. Look over the top edge of your racket at what's happening on the other side of the net.

Figure 1.6 Ready position.

Home Base

In singles, the base of operations after the ball has been put into play should be on or just behind the baseline at the center mark (figure 1.7). When in doubt, take that position and return to it after each shot. The base will change during rallies, depending on where you and your opponent hit the ball. In step 9 you will read about bisecting the angle of possible returns. That's another way of saying stand in the middle of where you think the ball is likely to be returned. For now, consider the spot at the middle of the baseline home base.

Footwork

You've already been through the preparation, swing, and follow-through sequence of moves for shots that come toward the forehand side of your body. On shots that move you out of position on the court, there are two ways to approach the bounce: the shuffle step and the crossover step.

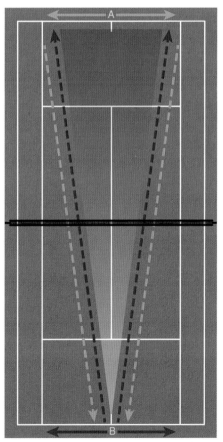

Figure 1.7 The middle of the baseline is home base between shots. It may change, depending on where you and your opponent hit the ball.

SHUFFLE STEP

To perform the shuffle step (figure 1.8), move laterally right or left, shuffling in the direction in which you want to go. While you're shuffling, get the racket back in a position to hit a forehand. Keep your hips low to the ground by bending at the knees slightly.

Figure 1.8 Shuffle step.

CROSSOVER STEP

The other method of moving to the ball is called a crossover step (figure 1.9). The crossover step is used to run for shots farther away. The technique is simple: Move to your right, pivot on your right foot, and then cross over with the left and take off. To move to your left, pivot on the left foot and cross in front with the right. It doesn't matter if you are right-handed or left-handed. The technique is the same.

Figure 1.9 Crossover step.

The following footwork drills will help improve your footwork. Once you are able to move quickly from side to side without even thinking about footwork, you are ready to concentrate on other fundamentals.

Forehand Drill 1   Grounders (two players)

To practice court coverage, start with grounders (figure 1.10). Stand at the center mark without a racket but in the ready position. A practice partner at the T (where the center service line intersects the service line) holds two tennis balls. Your partner rolls the balls alternately to your right and left sides (five to the right and five to the left). Using the shuffle step, move to the right to field the first grounder, roll it back to your partner, and shuffle to the left for the next ball.

Variation

A variation of grounders is the wave drill. Start at the center mark on the baseline. Have a partner or teacher stand 20 feet (6 m) in front and signal you to move forward, backward, right, or left. Carry the racket in the ready position and use the shuffle step to move right and left. Continue for 30 seconds; then change roles.

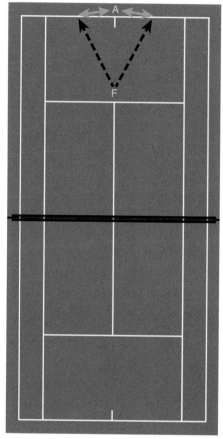

Figure 1.10 Grounders.

TO INCREASE DIFFICULTY
- The partner tosses grounders randomly to the right or left.
- The partner increases the speed of the ball.
- The partner increases the distance or angle between grounders.

TO DECREASE DIFFICULTY
- The partner tosses grounders only to one side.
- The partner slows the speed of the ball.
- The partner narrows the distance or angle between grounders.

(continued)

9

Forehand Drill 1   *(continued)*

Success Check

- Shuffle your feet sideways without crossing one over the other.
- Keep your hips low to the ground and your knees slightly bent.

1 point for every grounder fielded without a bobble

Your score: ___ out of 10

Forehand Drill 2
One-Bounce Catch (two players)

For the one-bounce catch drill, you and a partner take the same positions as in grounders (see figure 1.10). Instead of rolling grounders to you, your partner alternately tosses 10 balls so that they bounce to your right and left. Take a crossover step, move quickly, and catch the ball with one hand before it bounces a second time. Roll it back and recover for the next toss. Tosses may bounce at about waist height behind or in front of the baseline.

TO INCREASE DIFFICULTY
- The partner tosses balls randomly to the right or left.
- The partner increases the speed of tossed balls.
- The partner increases the distance or angle between tossed balls.

TO DECREASE DIFFICULTY
- The partner tosses balls only to one side.
- The partner slows the speed of tossed balls.
- The partner narrows the distance or angle between tossed balls.

Success Check

- Use a quick pivot and crossover step.
- Plant the outside foot; then push off for the next catch.

Score Your Success

1 point for every ball caught after one bounce

Your score: ___ out of 10

Forehand Drill 3
Shuffle–Crossover Step (one player)

Take a ready position in the middle of the service court. With your racket in hand, use a shuffle step to move past the singles sideline as fast as you can. Plant the outside foot, and use a crossover step to turn and run past the centerline. Return to the starting point and continue the same thing in the opposite direction until you've completed a total of 10 back-and-forth movements (figure 1.11).

TO INCREASE DIFFICULTY

- Don't stop between drill segments. Keep moving until you finish 10 sequences.
- Have a partner time the first segment. Try to match or break your speed record with each subsequent trial.

TO DECREASE DIFFICULTY

- Move at a slow-motion speed to practice the footwork.

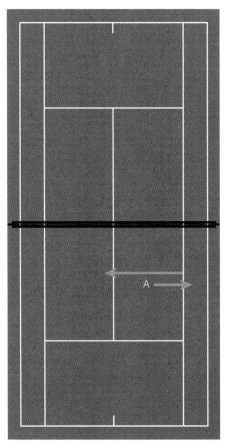

Figure 1.11 Shuffle–crossover step.

Success Check

- Stay low to maintain your center of gravity.
- Plant the outside foot to push off when changing directions.

Score Your Success

1 point for each perfect footwork sequence

Your score: ___ out of 10

Stance

There are four ways to position your feet when you hit a forehand—square, closed, semiopen, and open—and you'll probably use all of them sooner or later.

SQUARE

The square stance (figure 1.12), sometimes referred to as the neutral stance, is the most traditional and the one most often taught to beginners. As the ball comes to your forehand side, move into a position so that your feet and shoulders are somewhat parallel to the singles sideline. A right-handed player's left shoulder will point toward the net or the ball; a left-handed player's right shoulder will do the same. In other words, your entire body—upper body, trunk, and lower body—is approximately perpendicular to the net.

The main advantage of the square stance is that it allows the hitter to transfer weight into the shot. The disadvantage is that it takes time to set up perfectly, which is not always available in rapid exchanges. It's also harder to disguise the placement of your shot. By looking at your feet, smart players are able to know what you can and cannot do.

Figure 1.12 Square stance.

CLOSED

Assume the square stance ready position again. Now move the front foot another step toward the sideline. Instead of your feet forming an imaginary line parallel to the sideline, you have crossed over the line with your front foot. This position is the closed stance (figure 1.13).

You have no choice but to use the closed stance when you are hitting on the run or playing certain shots. The problem is the transfer of weight. When you step across instead of forward, it's virtually impossible to shift your weight in the direction you want to hit. Without a forward weight shift or a rotation of the hips, the power that you generate has to come from someplace else. It's a mistake to learn the closed stance as the standard for a beginner's forehand; but it is important to know what it is, when to use it, and why you're hitting in that position.

Figure 1.13 Closed stance.

SEMIOPEN

Go back to the square stance. This time instead of stepping closer to the sideline with the front foot, move the front foot slightly to the left and back a bit. This positioning opens your hips and shoulders more toward the net, placing you in the semiopen stance (figure 1.14).

Although you're giving up some of the forward weight-transfer capacity in this position, you can still generate power. The real advantage of the semiopen stance is that it offers court coverage options that the square and closed stances don't. The position of the left foot gives you a head start in court coverage of the open court. A quick recovery may not seem like a big deal, but saving a split second or a half step can mean the difference between winning and losing points.

The semiopen stance is used extensively by elite-level players who are

Figure 1.14   Semiopen stance.

baseline specialists. The combination of a semi-Western grip and a semiopen stance allows a player to swing hard and hit hard—a very appealing way to play the game.

Be aware of the semiopen stance, experiment with it, and use it if it fits your style. Some teachers prefer to teach the semiopen as the stance of choice for beginning players; most instructors, however, still start players with the square stance.

OPEN

One more time, use the square stance as a starting point. Now move to the semiopen stance, but don't stop there. Go all the way to an open stance, in which your feet and shoulders are parallel to the baseline and the net (figure 1.15). You can even use the ready position as a guide to where your feet should be. They are already in the correct position. Everything—shoulders, hips, and feet—is open to the net. In the open stance, a player swings without trying to line the feet up with anything. When the weight shifts in the open stance, the shift is to the outside foot. Power is generated by an explosive arm action and by rotating the hips with, not before, the swing.

Many tournament players use the open stance effectively with a semi-Western or Western grip. They can hit hard, disguise the direction of their shots, and be in a

Figure 1.15   Open stance.

great position to cover the court after a hit. The open stance is a good option when you don't have time to set up in another stance, when the ball comes at you directly, and when you have to move wide to hit a forehand.

The open stance versus the square stance debate among tennis players has been going on for decades. The arguments usually have fallen along age-group lines. Older players believe in the traditional stance (shoulders and feet parallel to the sidelines). Younger players and their teachers prefer a style with shoulders square to the net.

The arguments are simple enough. The square stance allows for a coordinated movement toward the target, a longer hitting zone, and greater racket speed. The advantages of the open stance are quicker recovery and better court coverage. Powerful, high-tech rackets somewhat offset the need to transfer body weight forward.

Reading about the way to hold a racket and move your feet takes more time than doing it. Everything happens in a hurry during a rally, so don't get discouraged by wordy explanations. You'll quickly reach a point in your training at which you do things without thinking about them first.

Forehand Drill 4
Footwork Scramble (two players)

Stand at the middle of the service line. Have a partner sit behind the net on the opposite side and toss 10 balls anywhere inside the two service courts (figure 1.16). Every time you make contact, the partner tosses another ball to a different area of the forecourt. Don't hit hard, and don't worry about forehand or backhand technique. Just concentrate on footwork, using any of the stances described.

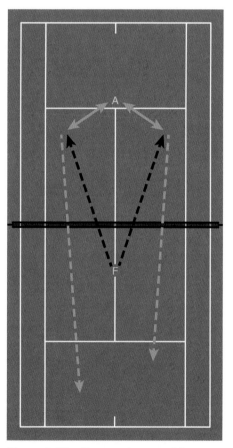

Figure 1.16 Footwork scramble.

Variation

For variety, have a partner stand at the net with a basket of balls and toss or hit 10 consecutive balls to your forehand side or down the middle of the court. Return each ball with a forehand to the opposite singles court. Increase difficulty, decrease difficulty, check your fundamentals, and score your success the same as in the original footwork scramble drill. Again, concentrate on footwork, not on stroke production.

TO INCREASE DIFFICULTY
- Hit every shot with a forehand regardless of where it is tossed.

TO DECREASE DIFFICULTY
- Have your partner feed balls only from the center service line to the singles sideline.

Success Check
- Use shuffle steps for close balls.
- Use crossover steps for balls that are farther away.
- Plant the outside foot to push off in the opposite direction.

Score Your Success
1 point for each ball returned into the singles court

Your score: ___ out of 10

Backswing

Beginning players can simplify the backswing by taking the racket straight back below the waist before bringing it straight forward to hit, similar to a door opening and closing. Very quickly, however, you'll develop your own unique backswing style. As long as you stay within some general guidelines, it's okay to develop your own style of backswing.

The first rule is to start getting the racket ready (and turning your shoulders) as soon as you know where the ball is going. Don't wait for the bounce on your side. The second rule is to find a backswing position that is neither too short nor too long. If you are a beginner, start by taking the racket back far enough to point it toward the back fence or wall. More experienced players may take the racket back farther in certain situations. If your backswing is short, you can't hit with as much power. If your backswing is too long, however, the margin of error increases. Besides, you don't always have time for a long backswing. The last rule is to develop an abbreviated looping motion with your racket—up, back, and then a slight hesitation before swinging forward to hit the ball. A diagram of the loop would look similar to a backward letter C (figure 1.17).

Figure 1.17 Backswing.

Forward Swing

Every drill up to this point has been done to get into a solid hitting position and to build, in segments, momentum for the forward swing. Now you're ready to hit. The forward swing is a chain reaction of movements that started with your footwork.

Taking a horizontal swing path with the racket face perpendicular to the court is okay for beginners. Even world-class players flatten the trajectories of their swings when they want to hit hard and flat.

Otherwise, the swing is forward and upward, brushing the back of the ball (figure 1.18). The more vertical the swing path is, the more topspin is put on the ball (figure 1.19). Topspin is good for control, consistency, and making the ball bounce high on the other side.

Figure 1.18 Forward swing.

Keep your head still, hold the racket with a firm grip, and make contact early. Wrist action is more significant in today's strokes than in the past. A traditional Eastern forehand grip requires a relatively fixed wrist position for most shots, but players who use a Western or semi-Western grip put a lot of stress on the wrist and forearm as they whip upward and across the back of the ball. Try to make contact before the ball reaches a position that is even with the midsection of your body. Some teachers advise hitting the ball a foot in front of the body. You can't always hit that far out in front, but do try.

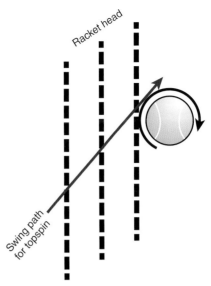

Figure 1.19   Swing path for topspin.

Forehand Drill 5   Forehand Setups (two players)

Stand behind the service line in the middle of the court, and have your practice partner toss 10 consecutive balls so that they bounce waist high to your forehand. Your objective is to return it with a forehand inside the singles court (figure 1.20).

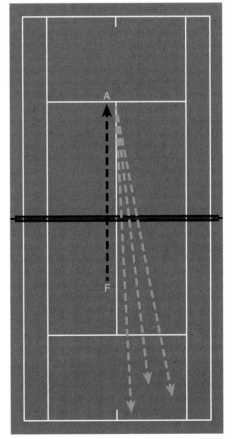

Figure 1.20   Forehand setups.

(continued)

Forehand Drill 5   *(continued)*

TO INCREASE DIFFICULTY

- Start the drill from the baseline.
- Have your partner increase the pace of the setups.
- Have your partner hit, rather than toss, setups.

TO DECREASE DIFFICULTY

- Have your partner reduce the pace of setups.
- Start with the racket back.
- Practice drop-and-hit forehands, with your partner dropping the ball on your forehand side.

Success Check

- Focus on control, not power.
- Use a horizontal or down-to-up swing.

Score Your Success

1 point for each successful forehand returned into the singles court

Your score: ___ out of 10

Forehand Drill 6
Drop-and-Hit Forehands (one player)

This drill helps you make contact with the ball before it gets past you. From the baseline, assume a square stance with the racket ready to swing forward. Drop 10 consecutive balls in front and to the side of your front foot where you are standing. Strike the ball approximately even with your front foot. Hit each ball a few feet over the net, as far as possible into the backcourt. Attempt to hit each shot into the opposite singles court. This drill is also the way to begin groundstroke exchanges during practice and warm-ups.

TO INCREASE DIFFICULTY

- Count only those shots that bounce in the opposite backcourt.
- Place and aim at targets.

TO DECREASE DIFFICULTY

- Move closer to the net to hit.
- Use larger targets.

Success Check

- Shift your weight forward when you swing.
- Make contact even with or in front of your front foot.

Score Your Success

1 point for each successful forehand hit into the singles court

Your score: ___ out of 10

Follow-Through

The way you finish a stroke depends on which stance and which grip you use. Semi-Western grips are associated with follow-throughs that wrap around the front of the body, even the neck (figure 1.21*a*). The Western grip follow-through is shorter, similar to a windshield-wiper motion (figure 1.21*b*). For the Eastern grip, the follow-through is upward, outward, and across (figure 1.21*c*).

Figure 1.21 Follow-through: *(a)* semi-Western grip; *(b)* Western grip; *(c)* Eastern grip.

All three follow-through methods ensure that you don't slow your swing down before making contact with the ball. Instructors often say, "Hit through the ball." When you do that, you're allowing for a normal slowdown of the racket head after contact with the ball. If you stop short, you'll probably hit the ball shorter without much power. You may also expose yourself to the risk of arm and shoulder injuries.

Check your follow-through by having your partner set you up with waist-high forehands. After each stroke, freeze at the end of your follow-through. Check the position of your racket against the guidelines just described.

Forehand Drill 7
Consecutive Forehands (two players)

Each player is on his or her baseline. Either player drops and puts a ball into play to the forehand side of the opposite court (figure 1.22). Try the drill five times, and count the number of total consecutive forehands hit by both players working as a team before making an error. Record the highest number out of 10. The idea is to control the ball with a moderately hit shot, not to hit the ball hard.

Variations

One variation of the consecutive forehands drill is the consecutive crosscourt forehands drill (figure 1.23). Execute the same drill, but direct all forehands crosscourt (forehand to forehand for right-handers). Shots that do not fall into the opposing crosscourt singles area are misses.

A second variation is the wall-ball forehand drill. Stand 20 feet (6 m) or less from a practice wall. Try to keep the ball in play against the wall with softly hit forehands. The idea is to control the ball with a moderately hit shot, not to hit the ball hard.

Finally, try the alleys-only variation (figure 1.24). Stand opposite your practice partner at the baseline behind the doubles alley. Keep the ball in play with forehands, and try to make all shots bounce in the alley across the net. This variation is very difficult and is better suited for intermediate and advanced players.

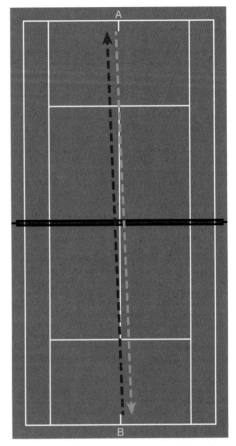

Figure 1.22   Consecutive forehands.

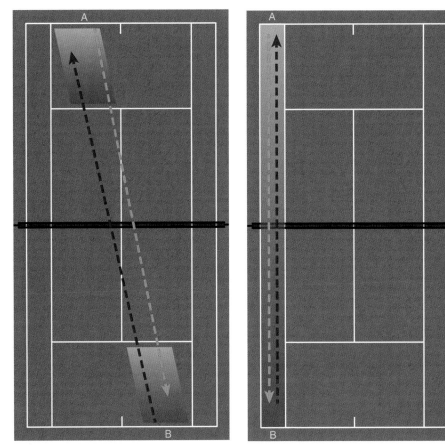

Figure 1.23 Consecutive crosscourt forehands.

Figure 1.24 Alleys-only forehands.

TO INCREASE DIFFICULTY

- Each player has to hit up to 10 consecutive forehands (20 total shots).

TO DECREASE DIFFICULTY

- When one player misses a shot, put another ball in play and continue the count for the player who has not made a mistake.
- Conduct the drill from the service lines instead of the baselines.

Success Check

- Prepare early.
- Make early contact.
- Complete the follow-through.

Score Your Success

1 point for each consecutive forehand hit into the singles court

Your score: ___ out of 10

Forehand Drill 8
Middle–Wide–Middle Forehands (two players)

Begin behind the baseline center mark with a partner or setter and a basket of balls at the net on the opposite side (figure 1.25). Your partner feeds the first ball wide to your forehand, but no farther than the singles sideline. Move to hit the first forehand feed; then immediately move back to the middle of the baseline to hit the next feed, also to your forehand. Continue returning balls alternately from a wide position and the middle position for 10 shots, hitting only forehands.

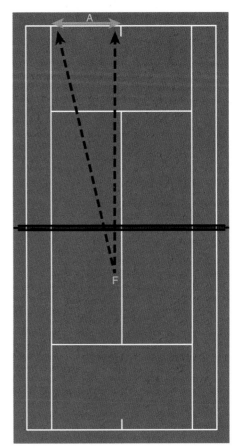

Figure 1.25   Middle–wide–middle forehands.

TO INCREASE DIFFICULTY
- The feeder hits balls with more velocity.
- The feeder hits balls that are harder to reach.
- The feeder increases the frequency of the balls hit.
- The feeder increases the number of balls from 10 to 13 to 15.

TO DECREASE DIFFICULTY
- The feeder hits balls with less velocity.
- The feeder hits balls that are easier to reach.
- The feeder decreases the frequency of the balls hit.
- The feeder decreases the number of balls from 10 to 8 to 6.

Success Check
- Use quick shuffle or crossover steps to move to the ball.
- Experiment with an open or semiopen stance when hitting (to recover quickly).
- Hit and immediately move, anticipating the next shot.

Score Your Success
1 point for each successful forehand hit into the singles court

Your score: _____ out of 10

Forehand Drill 9 **Forehand Games (two players)**

This drill is the final test of your forehand. From the baseline, put 10 balls into play against a partner's forehand on the opposite baseline. After the setup and return, play the point out. Every stroke has to be hit to your opponent's forehand and with your forehand. Restart the point when shots are not hit to a reasonable forehand position. Go for winners when you can.

TO INCREASE DIFFICULTY

- Play every shot with a forehand even if the ball goes to your backhand side.
- Increase the number of balls put into play to 11, 12, 13, 14, or 15.

TO DECREASE DIFFICULTY

- Loft the ball slightly to give each player more time.
- Keep the ball in play rather than trying to hit winners.

Success Check

- Maintain quick feet.
- Take the racket back early.
- Keep the wrist laid back.
- Make early contact.

Score Your Success

1 point for each point won

Your score: ___ out of 10

SUCCESS SUMMARY

Good players make tennis look easy because while we're watching the ball being hit on one end of the court, they are already preparing for the next shot on their end. For great forehands, stay busy with your feet. Use a shuffle or crossover step to move quickly to get into position, whether your stance is open, closed, semiopen, or square. Turn your shoulders, take the racket back, and use an abbreviated loop before hitting all the way through the ball.

Expect every shot to come back. As soon as you've hit a forehand—just like the great players do—use your off hand to adjust your grip and start getting into position for the next shot.

Enter the numbers you recorded in the Score Your Success section for each drill in the following scoring summary and add them to rate your forehand success. Your goal is 45 or more out of 90 possible points.

SCORING SUMMARY

FOREHAND DRILLS

1. Grounders   _____ out of 10
2. One-bounce catch   _____ out of 10
3. Shuffle–crossover step   _____ out of 10
4. Footwork scramble   _____ out of 10
5. Forehand setups   _____ out of 10
6. Drop-and-hit forehands   _____ out of 10
7. Consecutive forehands   _____ out of 10
8. Middle–wide–middle forehands   _____ out of 10
9. Forehand games   _____ out of 10

Total   _____ **out of 90**

Backhands: Developing a Weapon

The backhand is a challenge for some players, but it doesn't have to be. They are often defeated more by their mental backhand than by the actual backhand itself, which can be as good as their forehand.

Some coaches routinely tell their players, "Feed the backhand and starve the forehand" (of their opponents). With a positive attitude and the will to practice a few simple techniques, you can cause this strategy of your opponents to backfire. Make your backhand a weapon of choice and surprise. Then the coaches of your opponents will tell them to stay away from, or not to serve to, your backhand.

HITTING A BACKHAND

There are more ways to hold and swing the racket on a backhand than on a forehand, which gives you more freedom for variety. If you are new to tennis, you can experiment with two or three grips and swing patterns to find the ones most comfortable for your body and your style of play. If you've been playing for a while, it might be time to see whether a change can improve your backhand.

Too many players are satisfied if they simply develop a backhand that won't get them into trouble. As they get better, they begin to realize that the backhand can be just as effective for winning points as the forehand. Once you have a competent backhand, think in terms of controlling points with both groundstrokes, forehand and backhand. Develop winning groundstroke patterns. Make the other player expect a certain shot placement; then hit it to a different part of the court. Use backhand and forehand combinations to make your opponent cover more area. When you are in position for a winning forehand, backhand, volley, or any other shot, go for it! Specific suggestions for backhand tactics appear in steps 9 and 10.

Several of the footwork and forehand drills in step 1 can also be effective on the backhand side. The step 1 drills that apply equally to backhand practice are grounders, one-bounce catch, shuffle–crossover step, and footwork scramble. Tips for increasing and decreasing difficulty, checking your success, and scoring your success are similar to those in step 1.

One-Handed Backhand

The traditional grip for the one-handed backhand is the Eastern grip (figure 2.1). With this grip, a right-handed player's wrist should be slightly to the left of the top of the racket handle when looking down on the racket, with the racket edges perpendicular to the court. A left-handed player's wrist will be slightly to the right of the top. Think of your thumb as having a top, bottom, outside, and inside. The inside part of the thumb should be in contact with the back flat bevel of the racket handle. You can align your thumb in various positions along that part of the grip, but it is essential that the inside part be in contact with the racket. During a point, the thumb's position may change, but the part of the thumb that touches the grip should not.

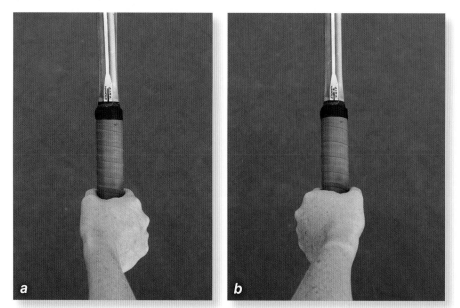

Figure 2.1   Eastern backhand grip: *(a)* for a right-handed player; *(b)* for a left-handed player.

You can experiment with the Continental grip (figure 2.2), but unless you have a very strong wrist and forearm, the grip won't work. With a Continental grip, the wrist is directly on top of the racket handle. The thumb has to provide more support from the rear because the wrist is not positioned behind the racket. Extend your thumb along the back of the grip so that the inside part is in contact and pushing against the racket handle during the stroke. If you use a Continental grip for the forehand (few players do), you won't have to change grips to hit a backhand. The disadvantage is that some players feel uncomfortable hitting shots this way on either side of the body because the Continental grip is halfway between the conventional Eastern forehand and backhand grips.

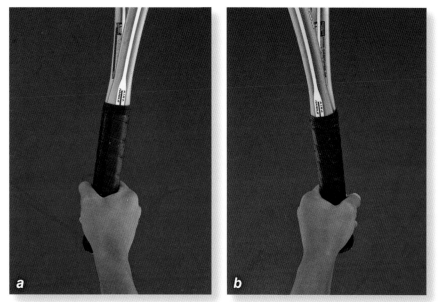

Figure 2.2   Continental backhand grip: *(a)* for a right-handed player; *(b)* for a left-handed player.

Regardless of how you hold the racket, start turning your shoulders and taking the racket back as soon as the ball leaves the other player's racket. Learn to prepare as you move to hit; don't delay. Use your off hand to lightly cradle the racket somewhere on the throat. Leave that hand to stabilize the throat during the entire backswing and as you adjust your grip after hitting every shot.

When hitting the one-handed backhand (figure 2.3), beginning players should take the racket back in a line horizontal to the ground at about waist height. Think of drawing a sword out of your side pocket. More advanced players can try to develop a small loop by bringing the racket back above the waist; then dropping it down below the back of the knee before swinging forward.

Figure 2.3 ONE-HANDED BACKHAND

Preparation

1. Eastern grip
2. Racket cradled at throat with opposite hand
3. Shoulder turn and racket back early
4. Square stance when time permits

Swing

1. Weight shifted forward
2. Parallel or low-to-high swing path
3. Early contact

Follow-Through

1. Outward
2. Across
3. Upward

MISSTEP

You are holding your arm too high.

CORRECTION

Position your arm at waist height or lower.

MISSTEP

You are holding the racket or racket head too high on the backswing.

CORRECTION

Think about pulling the racket out of a pocket on your shorts or skirt.

MISSTEP

Your knuckles on the racket hand are pointing to the sky.

CORRECTION

Your knuckles on the racket hand should be moving forward and pointing in the direction in which you want to hit.

Three of the stance options for the forehand are also options for the backhand. The closed stance is a necessity on some shots, but it is not recommended as the setup of choice. The semiopen stance is good for court coverage, but players using this stance may find it a little difficult to generate power. The ideal stance for the backhand is, time permitting, the square stance because it is good for transferring weight forward. A completely open stance is not an option for the one-handed backhand. Although the open stance is great for covering the court, it is only useful to players who use a two-handed backhand. Whatever stance you choose, be sure to spread your feet comfortably to establish a wide base for balance.

Beginning players should swing in a trajectory approximately parallel to the ground. Concentrate on taking the racket back in a straight line and swinging forward in a straight line, with a slight lift after contact. The follow-through is similar to that of an airplane taking off on a long runway. You can make changes to your backhand as your game develops. Intermediate players should take the racket back a little higher than the waist and then drop it down before swinging forward and upward through an imaginary tunnel. The body rotates into the shot, although the rotation is greater in the upper body and shoulders than it is in the hips. Visualize the path of both the backswing and the forward swing as a walking cane that is not parallel but instead tilted slightly up at the bottom, pointing toward the ball. A little hook at the back represents the miniloop backswing; the swing then continues in a straight line going up to the ball. The racket face should be perpendicular to the ground on contact.

Keep your wrist firmly in place throughout the swing. The racket head should be slightly higher than your wrist on all but very low shots. Try to make contact with the ball when it is at least even with, and preferably in front of, your front foot. Extend your arm comfortably when you swing. Find a comfort zone, and groove your swing through that zone in a consistent manner.

Follow through with the swing out toward the net, across the front of your body, and up, in that order. Think of reaching out for the net with the back of your hand and then bringing the racket up and across your upper body. Finish the stroke by pointing the racket generally in the direction of the target.

Two-Handed Backhand

Hitting a backhand with a two-handed grip is more common than hitting it with a one-handed grip. The two-handed backhand (figure 2.4) adds power, helps control the swing, and provides a better racket position to hit the ball with topspin. The two-handed backhand, however, is not for everyone. The disadvantages of this option include not being able to reach as far for wide shots, an inability to maneuver the racket easily on shots hit directly at the player, and the lack of strength development in the dominant arm.

Figure 2.4   TWO-HANDED BACKHAND

Preparation

1. Two Eastern forehand grips, an Eastern backhand grip combined with an Eastern forehand grip, or a Continental–Eastern grip combination

2. Quick upper-body turn

3. Open, semiopen, or square stance

Swing

1. Low-to-high swing path

2. Lift with legs

3. Body uncoils with swing

4. Ball contacted slightly in front of body

Follow-Through

1. Up

2. Out

3. Across

The two-handed backhand grip can be held in several ways. The simplest is to use an Eastern forehand grip with the dominant hand and add an Eastern forehand grip with the other hand (figure 2.5). The hands touch each other, and the fingers sometimes overlap or are spread along the racket grip. Some players prefer to use an Eastern backhand grip with the strong hand and an Eastern forehand grip with the other hand, whereas others use a Continental–Eastern grip combination.

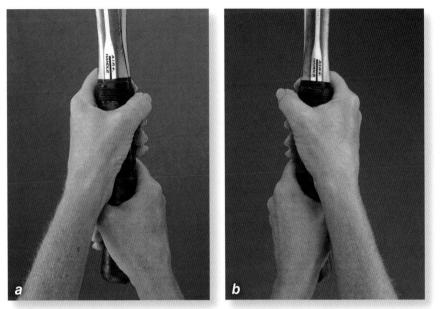

Figure 2.5   Two-handed backhand grip using two Eastern forehand grips: *(a)* for a right-handed player; *(b)* for a left-handed player.

Other grip combinations involving both hands can be used, but try not to get confused. If you use one hand to hit the backhand, make your first choice an Eastern forehand grip and support the racket on the throat with the opposite hand. If you use two hands, try using a Continental or Eastern backhand grip with the dominant hand. The second hand should take an Eastern or semi-Western forehand grip. From that starting point you can experiment with slight changes and find the combination of grips that is effective for you.

Use the dominant hand to make whatever grip change is needed quickly, and add your choice of grips with the other hand. While you're getting the right grip and turning your shoulders, you should be moving toward the path of the ball and getting ready to plant your feet. Take the racket back into a lower position before driving upward and forward to hit the ball with topspin. Put backspin on the ball by starting with the racket a bit higher than the waist and using a higher-to-lower swing path. Turn your hips and shoulders far enough to show your back to your opponent. Be ready to uncoil your body into the swing.

A closed stance is not a good position for hitting a two-handed backhand. Depending on the circumstances, position your feet to hit from a square stance, a semiopen stance (for a combination of power and court coverage), or an open stance (figure 2.6). Form a strong base of support by crouching slightly and spreading your feet wider than your shoulders. Players who use the two-handed backhand rely on the completely open stance to uncoil their bodies into the shot and to get a head start on recovering for the next return. Right-handed players take a step with the left foot around to the side after the swing for a push-off in the opposite direction. Left-handed players do the same with the right foot.

Figure 2.6 Stances for the two-handed backhand: *(a)* square, *(b)* semiopen, and *(c)* open.

The wrist action is more significant if you hit the backhand with two hands. Swing the racket in a downward-to-upward motion through the ball. Your arms will be closer to your body than they would be when hitting a one-handed backhand. Players who use effective two-handed backhands uncoil their bodies into the shot, starting with the hips. One of the advantages of the two-handed backhand is that you can hesitate to make contact. In fact, contact doesn't have to happen out in front. The follow-through will whip across the front of your body and may even wrap around your neck.

Backhand Drill 1
Backhand Setups (two players)

This drill is good for getting the feel of the backswing, whether one-handed or two-handed. Stand behind the service line in the middle of the court and have your partner toss 10 consecutive balls, bouncing them waist-high to your backhand (figure 2.7). The objective is to hit a return that lands inside the singles court.

TO INCREASE DIFFICULTY

- Start the drill from the baseline.
- Have your partner increase the pace of the setups.
- Have your partner hit, rather than toss, the setups.

TO DECREASE DIFFICULTY

- Have your partner reduce the pace of the setups.
- Start with the racket back.
- Practice drop-and-hit backhands, with your partner dropping the ball on your backhand side.

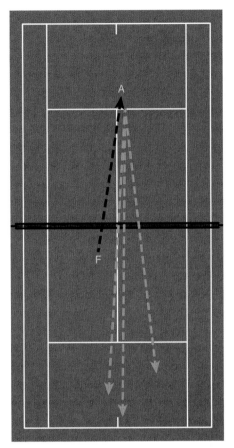

Figure 2.7   Backhand setups.

Success Check

- Focus on control, not power.
- Use a horizontal or low-to-high swing.

Score Your Success

1 point for each successful backhand returned into the singles court

Your score: ___ out of 10

Backhand Drill 2
Consecutive Backhands (two players)

The consecutive backhands drill offers another way to get used to holding and swinging the racket for a backhand stroke. Stand on or just behind the service line. Drop and softly put a ball into play to your partner's backhand (figure 2.8). Try the drill five times and count the number of consecutive soft-hit backhands, or backhand bumps, the two of you can hit before making an error. Record the highest number out of 10.

Variations

This drill has a couple of fun variations. For the consecutive baseline backhand variation, instead of playing from the service line, move back to your respective baselines and count the number of consecutive backhands in a rally. For the alleys-only variation, you and your practice partner stand on opposite ends of the court behind the doubles alley (see figure 1.24). Keep the ball in play with backhands, trying to make all shots bounce in the opposite alley or as near to it as possible.

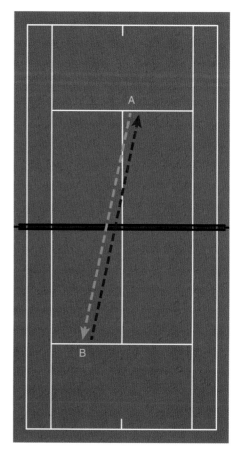

Figure 2.8   Consecutive backhands.

TO INCREASE DIFFICULTY
- Start the drill three steps behind the service line.
- Start the drill from the baseline (refer to the consecutive baseline backhand variation).

TO DECREASE DIFFICULTY
- Resume or add to the count after every missed shot instead of starting over.

Success Check
- Keep your off hand on the racket throat.
- Make a quick shoulder rotation.

Score Your Success
1 point for each consecutive backhand bump

Your score: ___ out of 10

Backhand Drill 3
Middle–Wide–Middle Backhands (two players)

Begin behind the baseline center mark with a partner or setter and a basket of balls at the net on the opposite side (figure 2.9). Your partner feeds the first ball wide to your backhand, but no farther than the singles sideline. Move to hit the first backhand feed; then immediately move back to the middle of the baseline to hit the next feed, also to your backhand. Continue returning balls alternately from a wide position and the middle position for 10 shots, hitting only backhands.

TO INCREASE DIFFICULTY

- The feeder hits balls with more velocity.
- The feeder hits balls that are harder to reach.
- The feeder increases the frequency of the balls hit.
- The feeder increases the number of balls from 10 to 13 to 15.

TO DECREASE DIFFICULTY

- The feeder hits balls with less velocity.
- The feeder hits balls that are easier to reach.
- The feeder decreases the frequency of the balls hit.
- The feeder decreases the number of balls from 10 to 8 to 6.

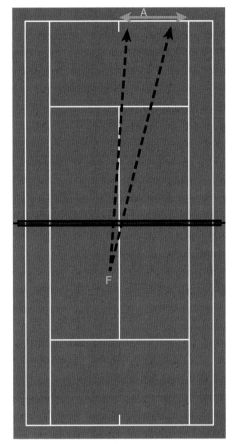

Figure 2.9 Middle–wide–middle backhands.

Success Check

- Use quick shuffle or crossover steps to move to the ball.
- Hit and immediately move, anticipating the next shot.

Score Your Success

1 point for each successful backhand hit into the singles court

Your score: _____ out of 10

Backhand Drill 4
Runaround Backhands (two players)

Position yourself at the baseline near the ad court doubles sideline (figure 2.10). Have your practice partner toss or set up a shot slightly toward your forehand side. Instead of returning the feed with your forehand, "run around" your forehand and return the shot with a backhand. As soon as you return the first shot, your partner feeds successive set-up balls (for a total of 10 feeds), each time tossing or setting up slightly toward your forehand until you've worked your way along the baseline from left to right as you face the net.

TO INCREASE DIFFICULTY

- The feeder hits balls with more pace.
- The feeder increases the frequency of the balls hit.
- The feeder increases the number of setups from 10 to 11, 12, or 13.

TO DECREASE DIFFICULTY

- The feeder hits balls with less velocity.
- The feeder decreases the frequency of the balls hit.
- The feeder decreases the number of setups from 10 to 9, 8, or 7.

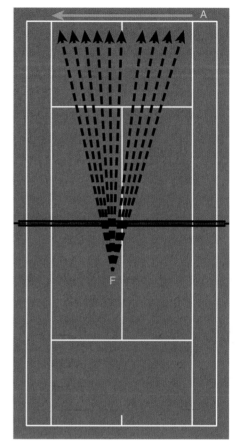

Figure 2.10 Runaround backhands.

Success Check

- Make a quick return to the ready position after each shot.
- Keep your feet moving throughout the drill.

Score Your Success

1 point for each successful backhand hit into the singles court

Your score: _____ out of 10

Backhand Drill 5
Backhand Games (two players)

From the baseline, put 10 balls into play to a partner's backhand on the opposite baseline. After the setup and return, play the point out. Every stroke has to be hit to your opponent's backhand using your backhand. Restart the point when shots are not hit to a reasonable backhand position. Go for winners when you can.

TO INCREASE DIFFICULTY

- Play every shot with a backhand even if the ball goes to your forehand side.
- Increase the number of balls put into play to 11, 12, 13, 14, or 15.

TO DECREASE DIFFICULTY

- Loft the ball slightly to give each player more time.
- Keep the ball in play rather than trying to hit winners.

Success Check

- Move your feet quickly between shots.
- Prepare your racket early.
- Complete the follow-through.

Score Your Success

1 point for each point won

Your score: ___ out of 10

Backhand Drill 6
Two-Minute Drill (two players)

Now it's time to combine forehand and backhand groundstrokes. Start the two-minute drill at the baseline. Return balls tossed randomly to your forehand and backhand sides nonstop for a period of two minutes. Count the number of "in" shots in segments of 10 attempts. Restart the count after 10 shots, but continue the drill for two minutes. Record your highest score.

TO INCREASE DIFFICULTY

- Return every shot with a forehand (or every shot with a backhand), regardless of where it's tossed.
- Return every shot (backhands and forehands) to the backhand side of your practice partner.
- Return every shot (backhands and forehands) to the backhand side of your practice partner beyond the service line.
- Have your partner hit, rather than toss, setups.

TO DECREASE DIFFICULTY

- Have your partner alternately toss to your forehand and backhand.
- Have your partner toss to the same side with every ball.

Success Check

- Don't watch your shot after striking it.
- Shorten your backswing when rushed.
- Maintain a "get-to-everything" attitude.

Score Your Success

1 point for each successful groundstroke in any 10-shot sequence

Your score: ___ out of 10

Backhand Drill 7
Groundstroke Games (two players)

To test your groundstrokes in a competitive situation, drill with groundstroke games. From the baseline, either player puts 10 balls into play anywhere in the opposite backcourt. After the setup and return, play the point out hitting forehands and backhands. Go for winners when you can.

TO INCREASE DIFFICULTY
- Exchange four consecutive groundstrokes before a point begins.
- Score a point only when you force your opponent to make an error.

TO DECREASE DIFFICULTY
- Score 2 points when you force your opponent to make an error.

Success Check
- After each shot, recover to the middle of the baseline (or to a point midway between the angle of possible returns).
- Make early contact on forehands.
- "Build points" to set up a winning situation.

Score Your Success

1 point for each point won

Your score: ___ out of 10

SUCCESS SUMMARY

At most skill levels, the player who can keep the ball in play four or five times during a point has a greater chance to win. The immediate goal for the backhand is consistency. Once you can put the backhand where you want it consistently, start working on more pace. The keys are quick footwork, upper-body rotation during preparation, and a smooth but strong swing all the way through the ball. Experiment with a variety of one-handed and two-handed grips and decide which one is right for you. Find a groove so you don't even have to think about the mechanics of hitting the shot. Make contact early. In your mind, determine that nothing your opponent hits can get past you.

Enter the numbers you recorded for each drill in the following scoring summary. Add them to rate your backhand success. Your goal is 35 or more out of 70 possible points.

SCORING SUMMARY

BACKHAND DRILLS

1.	Backhand setups	_____ out of 10
2.	Consecutive backhands	_____ out of 10
3.	Middle–wide–middle backhands	_____ out of 10
4.	Runaround backhands	_____ out of 10
5.	Backhand games	_____ out of 10
6.	Two-minute drill	_____ out of 10
7.	Groundstroke games	_____ out of 10
Total		_____ **out of 70**

Serves: Taking the Offensive

So far, you've worked on groundstrokes—forehands and backhands. But every time you hit a groundstroke, it is a response to a shot hit by your opponent. In fact, every stroke in tennis except one, the serve, is influenced by how and where your opponent has hit the previous shot.

With the serve, you get to hit the first shot in every other game. A strong, consistent, well-placed serve is the first step toward taking the offensive. It can set you up to win points, games, and matches with your other strokes. A weak or inconsistent serve allows your opponent to take away that advantage. It's all up to you—completely under your control. Your opponent has to deal with it.

Players, teachers, coaches, tennis fans, and television announcers use the terms *hold serve* and *break serve*. You are expected to hold serve—to win games in which you are the server—because you are getting the first shot to start the point. The guaranteed formula for winning a tennis match is this: During each set, hold serve every time and break your opponent's serve once. You win.

It's not a magic number, but getting 60 percent of first serves in play is a reasonable goal. When the pros get their first serves in, they win the point about 75 percent of the time. They serve down the center to take advantage of the lower net and reduce the angle of an opponent's return. They serve to the backhand side if an opponent has a weak backhand. They serve deep to keep an opponent from closing and attacking their serves. And they serve wide to either side to open up the court for the next shot. You don't have to be a pro to begin doing the same thing with your serves. For tactics in specific situations and against certain kinds of opponents, read steps 9, 10, and 11.

HITTING A SERVE

You will eventually be able to do four things with your serve. The first is to get it into play consistently while using proper technique. At the beginning stage, technique is more important than consistency. Even if your serve is a bit inconsistent at the beginning, good technique will produce a better serve in the long run.

When you are able to consistently get your serve in play, the next goal is to place the ball wherever you want it to go within the opponent's service court:

1. Straight at your opponent

2. Down the middle of the court

3. Wide to the left or right side

4. Deep into the service court

The third objective is to hit more powerful serves. Power comes with increased strength and improved coordination as you prepare, swing, and follow through.

The last objective is to be able to hit with a variety of spins. This step will show you how to hit slice, topspin, and flat serves.

Once you can get serves into the service court, to a specific area of that court, with power, and with spin, you're no longer a beginner or an intermediate server. Now, you're an advanced player—at least when serving.

It's more difficult for beginners to hold serve because they haven't had enough time to develop it into an offensive tool. Now is the time to start. The following explanations, illustrations, and drills will help you develop a serve, beginning with the punch serve for beginners and continuing to an intermediate and advanced full-swing serve that can be used at any level of the game. Intermediate and advanced players can skip the punch serve section.

Punch Serve

Hold the racket with an Eastern forehand grip for the punch serve (figure 3.1). As your serving motion becomes more fluid, change to a Continental or modified Continental grip.

Stand behind the baseline at about a 45-degree angle to the net, facing one of the net posts. If you are right-handed, position your left foot forward at a 45-degree angle; if you are left-handed, position and angle your right foot forward. The foot away from the baseline should be placed so that an imaginary line drawn along the toes of both feet points in the direction in which you want to serve. Within reason, the exact alignment of the feet is a matter of individual preference.

To toss the ball, hold it at the base of your fingers. Extend your arm, holding the ball in the direction in which you want to hit, and lift the ball without bending very much at the elbow. As you lift, release the ball at eye level by opening your fingers. The ball should go up with little or no spin. Toss the ball so it reaches a peak higher than you can reach with your racket. Work on tossing the ball to the same spot consistently. You will not toss the ball perfectly every time, but developing a reliable toss will be one less thing that can go wrong. The target tosses drill will help you develop a groove (pattern) in your tossing motion.

Figure 3.1 **PUNCH SERVE**

Preparation

1. Eastern forehand grip
2. Body facing net post
3. Tossing arm extended forward
4. Racket behind head
5. Weight on back foot
6. Ball toss out and forward

Swing

1. Forward lean
2. High reach to hit
3. Wrist flop on contact

Follow-Through

1. Continued swing after hit
2. Out toward net
3. Down
4. Across

MISSTEP

The serve is short.

CORRECTIONS

Don't let the ball drop too low during the toss.
Increase racket head speed.

MISSTEP

The serve lacks control.

CORRECTIONS

Increase the number of practice repetitions.
Stand inside the baseline to serve during practice sessions.
Keep your wrist from unnecessary wobbling.
Reduce the velocity of the serve.

Take the racket to a position behind your back and touch the middle of your back with the top edge of your racket. Lift the racket head a few inches, or centimeters, and make this your starting point. Swing upward at the ball. The serve motion goes up before it goes forward. Don't let your elbow lead the stroke; keep it up until after the hit. When you hit, reach as high and as far out as you comfortably can. Your arm and racket should be fully extended when contact is made. With the hit, "flop" (pronate) your wrist. Turn it down and away on contact. After contact, continue to bring the racket forward toward the net and then down and across.

The swing to serve a tennis ball is not exactly like the throwing motion, but it has many things in common with throwing a baseball or softball. If you can throw well, you will probably serve well. To assess your throwing ability, try the ready, aim, throw drill.

Serve Drill 1 Target Tosses (one player)

Take a position behind the baseline. Extend your arm and racket up and forward to gauge the proper height. Practice 10 consecutive service tosses (figure 3.2). Let the ball drop to the court. Points count when the ball falls just inside the baseline.

Figure 3.2 Target tosses.

TO INCREASE DIFFICULTY
- Place a small towel or other target a few inches, or centimeters, inside the baseline and count only those tosses that hit the target.

TO DECREASE DIFFICULTY
- Use a bigger target.

Success Check

- Begin the tossing movement in the shoulder joint.
- Extend your fingers with the toss.
- Follow the ball with your hand and eyes.

1 point for each successful toss

Your score: ___ out of 10

Serve Drill 2 **Ready, Aim, Throw (one player)**

Stand at the baseline of one court near the center mark. Attempt to throw 10 consecutive balls diagonally into the opposite service court.

TO INCREASE DIFFICULTY
- Change positions along the baseline with each throw.
- Start from a position one or two steps behind the baseline.

TO DECREASE DIFFICULTY
- Start from a position one or two steps behind the service line.
- Count tosses that land anywhere in the opposite singles court.

Success Check

- Place the opposite shoulder and hip toward the net to start the motion.
- Step in the direction of the throw with the opposite foot.
- Take the throwing arm down and back, bend it, and extend it up and forward.
- Reach high to release.

Score Your Success

1 point for each successful throw

Your score: ___ out of 10

Serve Drill 3   Service-Line Serves (one player)

Put the entire serving motion into action by serving 10 consecutive balls into the proper service court, but serve from a position behind the service line instead of the baseline (figure 3.3). Practice serves from both the right and left sides of the service line.

TO INCREASE DIFFICULTY

- Move back to a position half-way between the service line and the baseline.
- Serve five times from the deuce court and five times from the ad court.

TO DECREASE DIFFICULTY

- Move forward to a position inside the service line.

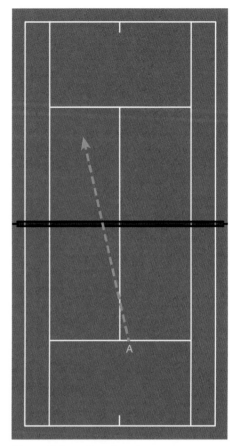

Figure 3.3   Service-line serves.

Success Check

- Start with the racket behind your head or back.
- Toss higher than you can reach.
- Reach high to hit.
- Keep your head up on contact.

Score Your Success

1 point for each successful serve

Your score: ___ out of 10

Serve Drill 4   **Area 51 (one player)**

Place a piece of tape across the service court to divide it into two halves, front and back (figure 3.4). Stand behind the baseline near the center mark and serve 10 consecutive balls into the area between the tape and the service line.

Variations

For variety, try long-distance serves. Instead of serving from the baseline position, serve from a position two steps behind the baseline. Another variation is called target practice. Place a large cardboard box or similar target deep and in the middle of the service court. Count the number of times your serve hits the target. Move the targets into the service-court corners to make the drill even more difficult (figure 3.5).

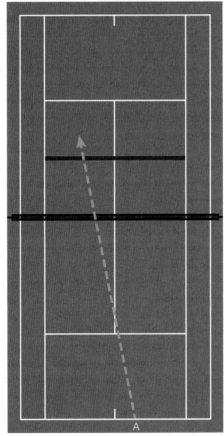

Figure 3.4   Area 51.

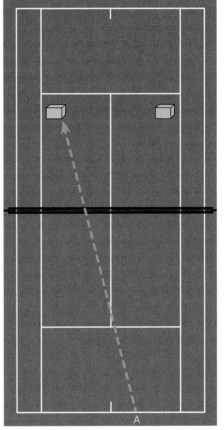

Figure 3.5   Target practice.

(continued)

Serve Drill 4   *(continued)*

TO INCREASE DIFFICULTY

- Use tape to divide the back service area into two parts, and serve alternately into each target area.
- Use a tennis ball can as the target.

TO DECREASE DIFFICULTY

- Move the tape closer to the net to allow a larger target area.
- Serve from a position between the baseline and service line.

Success Check

- Aim deep.
- Reach high to hit.
- See the contact between the racket strings and the ball.

Score Your Success

1 point for each serve into the designated target area

Your score: ___ out of 10

Serve Drill 5
Serve and Return Games (two players)

Play 10 points against a practice opponent using only the serve and return of serve. The server earns 1 point for every "in" serve. The receiver gets a point for every successful return. Change from right to left sides on the baseline after 5 points.

TO INCREASE DIFFICULTY (FOR THE SERVER)

- Give yourself only one chance to put each ball into play, rather than using the usual first serve, second serve routine.

TO DECREASE DIFFICULTY (FOR THE SERVER)

- Serve all 10 attempts from the same position.
- Stand one step inside the baseline to serve.

Success Check

- Concentrate on your serve, not the opponent's return.
- Make mistakes long (beyond the opposite service line), not short (into the net).
- Serve for consistency, not power.

Score Your Success

FOR THE SERVER:
1 point for each "in" serve

Server's score: ___ out of 10

FOR THE RECEIVER:
1 point for each successful return

Receiver's score: ___ out of ___ attempts

Full-Swing Serve

Intermediate and advanced players can use the full-swing serve (figure 3.6) to put the ball in play. Rather than just aiming at targets, imagine yourself in game situations in which you are ahead 40-30 and poised to win a game (or set) with a strong serve, or down 30-40 and in danger of losing a match with a weak serve or double fault.

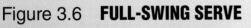

Figure 3.6 **FULL-SWING SERVE**

Preparation

1. Continental grip
2. Feet at 45-degree angle to net
3. Toss slightly higher than you could normally reach with the tip of an extended racket

Swing

1. Full down, back, up, and forward motion (some advanced players abbreviate the backswing)
2. Full extension of body, arm, and racket on contact
3. Forward weight shift
4. Wrist flop on contact

Follow-Through

1. Out
2. Slightly down
3. Across

MISSTEP

The serve lacks power.

CORRECTION

Pronate the wrist on contact with the ball.

MISSTEP

The toss is too far back (not inside the plane of the baseline) and out of the swing path.

CORRECTION

Toss the ball slightly forward in the direction in which you want to hit.

MISSTEP

The serve goes into the net.

CORRECTIONS

Keep your head up as you strike the ball.
Visualize the serve landing deep in the opposite service court.

Hold the racket with a Continental grip, although you may want to modify with an Eastern forehand to hit the ball flatter (without spin) or with an Eastern backhand to create a topspin effect. With the Continental grip, the wrist is directly over the top of the racket handle as you look down on it.

Position your feet at a 45-degree angle to the net, spread more than shoulder-width apart. Turn your side to the net and slightly bend your back knee as if coiling your body. Rotate and uncoil your body toward the ball with the swing. The angle at which you stand may vary a few degrees in either direction, depending on your preference.

To swing, start with your weight forward. Point your racket toward the target at about chest height, with your free hand holding the ball and touching the racket. Drop your racket head in a pendulum motion with the racket head passing by your legs. Some experienced players modify the downswing and backswing, creating an abbreviated motion. Move the ball slightly downward toward the front thigh before the toss at the same time the racket goes down. Again, some advanced players may delay the tossing or swinging movement to establish their own rhythm, but moving the hands down together and then up together is a good starting point. Drop the racket arm down, and in a continuous motion, move it up into the back-scratching position. Simultaneously move the other arm up to lift the ball for the toss. The service motion should have a rhythmic feel.

Time the toss so that the ball drops to a point above your head and slightly in front of your body at the same time you extend your racket arm to make contact. If the timing is way off, stop and reset the service motion from the beginning. The toss has to be far enough in front of you to force you to lean forward and beyond the baseline as you hit. Keep your head up and look at the ball while you are tossing.

To make the most of the weight transfer, move only the back foot during the motion. As you lean forward, keep the foot closer to the baseline in the same place, but move your other foot forward to meet it. Some players prefer to take one step, starting with the rear foot several inches (or centimeters) behind the baseline and finishing one step inside the line. Other players take a two-step approach with the rear foot, bringing the back foot forward to a point just behind the front foot prior to hitting. This movement results in a springboard effect and may even supply added height and leverage if you get up on your toes to hit.

Whether you employ a one-step or two-step approach with the back foot, bend your knees while preparing to hit. Part of the uncoiling motion of the body includes exploding upward from a knees-flexed to a knees-extended position. Not only are you turning into the ball, but you are also springing up to unleash the chain of events that starts with your feet and continues through the pronation of the wrist as you make contact with the ball.

As you bring the racket up and behind your back, your arm should begin to bend at the elbow and move through the back-scratching position. Extend your arm fully to make contact with the ball. When you strike the ball, your body should be almost in a straight line from your toes to your racket hand at the moment of impact. Advanced players pronate the wrist on contact with the ball to generate maximum power. Pronation means turning or rotating the thumb down and away from the body.

After you hit the ball, let your back foot continue to move forward, touching down on the court inside the baseline. The follow-through of the arm after the wrist snap will take care of itself, usually finishing the stroke down and across.

DEVELOPING A PRE-SERVE ROUTINE

Question: What do basketball players do before shooting a free throw? What do golfers do before teeing off or putting? What do hitters in baseball do to get ready for the next pitch?

Answer: They all go through a routine. It's different in every sport and it varies from player to player, but all athletes need to get into a comfortable zone, and they should do whatever they think is necessary to get there.

Beginning or inexperienced tennis players may not have a pre-serve routine. They set up to serve a different way every time, making each serve a new experience. Instead of preparing to hit 10 serves with one consistent setup, they prepare to hit 10 serves 10 different ways. The value of repetition is lost.

Experienced players have a routine. They might position their feet in a certain way, bounce or dribble the ball a few times, take a deep breath, or do all three before each serve.

What you do is not important (as long as it doesn't affect your serve in a negative way), but doing *something* to get into that performance zone is. Develop your particular pre-serve routine. If it doesn't seem to be working, change it.

Serve Drill 6
Consecutive First Serves (one player)

To assess your serve's effectiveness, attempt 10 consecutive first serves. Change from the deuce court to the ad court after the first five serves. Count a point for each successful serve.

TO INCREASE DIFFICULTY

- Alternate serving from deuce and ad positions with every serve.
- Serve only to a right-handed player's backhand side of the service court.

TO DECREASE DIFFICULTY

- Attempt all 10 serves from the same position.

Success Check

- Use a Continental grip.
- Toss in front of your body higher than the extended racket.

Score Your Success

1 point for each successful serve

Your score: ___ out of 10

Serve Drill 7
Serve and Return Games, Advanced (two players)

Play 10 points against a partner using only the serve and service return. The server gets a point for each serve in play. The receiver gets a point for each successful return. Change from right to left sides on the baseline after 5 points.

TO INCREASE DIFFICULTY

- Allow the server only one chance to put the ball into play, rather than allowing the usual first serve, second serve routine.

TO DECREASE DIFFICULTY

- Allow the server to stand inside the baseline.
- Allow the server two chances to put the serve into play.

Success Check

- Concentrate on your serve, not your opponent's return.
- Aim deep; make mistakes long, not short.
- Focus on consistency, not power.

Score Your Success

FOR THE SERVER:

1 point for each "in" serve

Server's score: ___ out of 10

FOR THE RECEIVER:

1 point for each successful return

Receiver's score: ___ out of ___ attempts

Serve Drill 8   Area 51, Advanced (one player)

Place a strip of tape across the service court to divide it into two halves, front and back. Place another strip of tape to divide the back area of the service court, right and left (see figure 3.7). Serve 10 consecutive balls—5 to the right target area and 5 to the left target area. Record the number of "in" serves.

TO INCREASE DIFFICULTY

- Use tape to divide the service court into three target areas (forehand corner, backhand corner, and middle), and serve alternately into each area.
- Use a tennis ball can as a target.

TO DECREASE DIFFICULTY

- Move the tape closer to the net to create a larger target area.

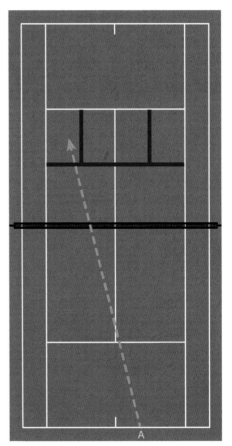

Figure 3.7   Area 51, advanced.

Success Check

- Visualize each serve hitting the target area.
- Maintain racket-head speed throughout the motion.

Score Your Success

1 point for each serve into the designated target area

Your score: ___ out of 10

SLICE SERVE

The point of contact between the racket and the ball varies depending on the kind of spin you want to put on the ball. For an extreme slice serve, a right-handed player tosses the ball wider and lower to the right than on a conventional serve. The racket strings strike the ball more to the side—at 2:00 or 3:00 instead of 1:00, when imagining the ball as the face of a clock (figure 3.8). Think of scraping your racket face around the edge of the ball.

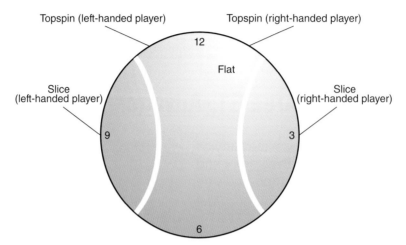

Figure 3.8   Where to strike the ball for flat, slice, and topspin serves.

TOPSPIN SERVE

To serve with topspin, toss the ball almost directly overhead. The racket brushes upward behind the ball from 7:00 in the direction of 1:00 (see figure 3.8). Contact is farther back than in a normal serving motion. Topspin serves should clear the net 2 or 3 feet (60-90 cm) higher than the flat serve. To achieve a topspin effect, change your grip from a Continental to an Eastern backhand.

Slice and topspin work well on second serves. The racket speed is the same or even faster than on first serves, but the angle at which the racket contacts the ball imparts spin, creating a greater margin of error and a safer service attempt.

FLAT SERVE

To hit a flat, hard serve, some players change from the Continental grip to an Eastern grip. Instead of trying to put sidespin or topspin on the ball, they position the wrist so the face of the racket strikes the ball in the middle of the clock face (see figure 3.8).

Serve Drill 9   Play a No-Ad Set (two players)

Now that you can hit serves and groundstrokes, it's time to play tennis. Play a set using no-ad scoring. The first player to win 4 points wins each game. If the score in a game is 3-3, the receiver has the option of receiving the serve from either the left or right side. Do the best you can if you have to hit volleys. Volleys are covered in step 4.

TO INCREASE DIFFICULTY

- Allow the opponent the choice of the right or left side on all points.
- The server gets only one attempt on each service point.

TO DECREASE DIFFICULTY

- The server chooses the right or left side on all points.
- The server gets three attempts on each service point.
- Begin serving the set.
- Use all second serves.

Success Check

- Eliminate double faults.
- Increase the "in play" percentage of first serves.

Score Your Success

1 point for each game won

Your score: ___ out of a maximum of 6 games

Serve Drill 10   **Play a Set (two players)**

Play a set using conventional scoring. Spin the racket in the hands to determine side and first serve. Change ends of the court every time the total number of games is an odd number.

TO INCREASE DIFFICULTY

- The server gets only one attempt on each service point.

TO DECREASE DIFFICULTY

- The server gets three attempts on each service point.

Success Check

- Concentrate on holding serve.
- Extend fully on service contact.
- Snap your wrist at the top of the swing.

Score Your Success

1 point for each game won

Your score: ___ out of a maximum of 6 games

RETURNING A SERVE

If your opponent is serving from the deuce court, stand on the right side of the court as you face the net on or slightly in front of the baseline, near the singles sideline (figure 3.9a). When your opponent serves from the ad court, stand slightly in front of the baseline on the left side of the court near the opposite singles sideline (figure 3.9b).

As in returning other shots in tennis, the idea is to position yourself in the middle of an extreme angle to which your opponent can serve. If your opponent has a weak first serve or a second serve with less pace, move forward a step or two before the service motion. Against a faster serve, especially on a fast court, play farther back to give yourself more time to react.

A beginning player serves with less pace, so return the serve just as you would return any other groundstroke. Watch your opponent's racket face when she is serving. As soon as you determine whether the ball is coming to your forehand or backhand, adjust your grip. If you are holding a forehand grip and the serve comes to the forehand side, no adjustment is necessary. If the serve comes to the other side, however, change to either the Eastern or two-handed backhand grip.

Move to the ball, and while turning your shoulders, get your racket back early. If you have time, step forward and swing in a parallel-to-the-court or slightly upward motion. Play against the ball, not your opponent. Concentrate on the service return as if you were returning forehands or backhands in a groundstroke drill. The idea is to put the ball in play and quickly get into a

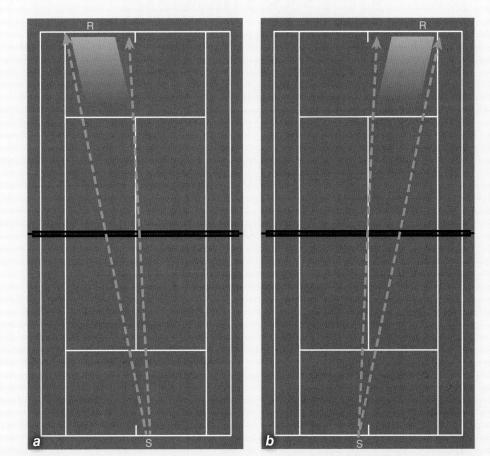

Figure 3.9 Returning the serve: *(a)* from the deuce court; *(b)* from the ad court.

position to win the point. If you can control the ball, think crosscourt, high over the net, and deep to your opponent's backcourt.

Returning an advanced serve presents a new combination of challenges. The ball comes faster than a groundstroke or a beginner's serve, leaving less time to prepare. Be extra alert to return a hard-hit serve. Get into the ready position, racket forward, body weight on the balls of your feet, and leaning forward. Many players take a short hop (or split step) just as the opponent strikes the ball. This movement puts the body into motion for a quick reaction.

You may not have time to set up in a traditional square stance to transfer your weight forward. If this is the case, turn your shoulders and shorten your backswing. Insufficient time also may not allow you to take the full, looping swing many players use to return groundstrokes. If you have time, however, go ahead and step forward quickly with the opposite foot.

Finally, do not fight power with power. If your opponent serves hard, hold your racket tightly and block the shot (return the ball with a very short swinging motion). Rebound the pace provided by the serve. If the ball comes at a slower pace, then you can go back to your normal preparation and supply the power yourself.

As the practice partner, you can use serve drills 6, 7, 8, 9, and 10 to practice the return of serve.

Tennis: Steps to Success

SUCCESS SUMMARY

The fundamentals for both beginner and intermediate serves are remarkably similar. Position the front foot at a 45-degree angle to the net. Toss higher than you can reach. Extend your body, arm, and racket fully to make contact with the ball. To get more power, increase the speed of the racket head and snap the wrist at contact.

For beginners, total the points you earned in drills 1 through 5 in the following scoring summary. If you scored 25 or more out of 50 possible points, you're ready to work on a full-swing serve.

Intermediate and advanced players enter the number of points scored in drills 6 through 10 in the scoring summary. Your goal is perfection, but 25 out of 42 (60 percent) is okay for now.

SCORING SUMMARY

SERVE DRILLS

Punch Serve Drills

1. Target tosses	_____ out of 10
2. Ready, aim, throw	_____ out of 10
3. Service-line serves	_____ out of 10
4. Area 51	_____ out of 10
5. Serve and return games	_____ out of 10
Total (for beginning players)	**_____ out of 50**

Full-Swing Serve Drills

6. Consecutive first serves	_____ out of 10
7. Serve and return games, advanced	_____ out of 10
8. Area 51, advanced	_____ out of 10
9. Play a no-ad set	_____ out of 6
10. Play a set	_____ out of 6
Total (for advanced players)	**_____ out of 92**

58

Volleys: Forcing the Action

If you like action, you will love volleying. The ball is hit before a bounce, and because you are moving closer to the net, you will have less time to react to your opponent's shots. Volleys help you to force the action and take control of the point. If your personality has an aggressive side, volleys let you express it. They also give you one more weapon for your opponent to worry about, which makes playing tennis even more fun.

Tennis players have to hit serves, forehands, and backhands to play the game, but in most singles situations they are not forced to hit volleys. Using a volley as an offensive weapon is a choice—a mind-set and a skill set. You have to want to get into a position in which you can hit volleys instead of depending solely on your ground-strokes to win points.

Having the ability to return shots from any position on the court, before or after the bounce, means you are no longer just a baseline player. You are now an all-court player.

Some players are so good at hitting groundstrokes from the baseline (or their rackets are so powerful) that they can win without good volleying skills. For all-court players, volleys become part of an offensive and defensive game plan. Why not enjoy having one more good shot?

In this step and in steps 9 and 10, you will read about situations that give you an advantage if you get to the net during a rally. Against which kind of opponent are volleys the most effective? When, during a rally, do you decide to use a volley? What kind of shot do you hit to put yourself in a position to hit a volley? And what should you expect your opponent to do after you've hit a volley?

Don't be satisfied with merely "hitting" a volley. Learn to hit it with pace and direction. A weak volley may cause you to lose the point on the next shot. A strong volley sets you up to win the point on the next shot.

Volleys are not important to all players in singles, but in doubles, volleys are a necessity for everyone. Good doubles teams get to the net early during a rally and often during a match. The net is where most points are won or lost. Timid players who don't play the net well or stay back on the baseline are always on the defensive. They allow the other team to force the action.

The technique for hitting volleys is very different from the technique used for groundstrokes. You'll use a different grip, hold your arm at a different angle, take a shorter backswing, and finish with an abbreviated follow-through. The following section explains how.

HITTING A VOLLEY

The ready position for a volley is the same as that for groundstrokes, except that your racket head is higher. With your chin up, you should be able to see just above the top edge of your racket (figure 4.1). Don't split your eyesight (one eye on each side of the racket edge); never allow the racket to distort your vision.

When you are close to the net, your opponent's shot arrives sooner, and there is not enough time to take your racket back very far. The backswing on both the forehand and backhand sides should be a short, restricted motion. As you see the ball coming, take your racket back to a point not much farther than an imaginary line even with your front shoulder and parallel to the net. The back to the wall drill forces you to volley with a short backswing.

Figure 4.1 Volley ready position.

Volley Drill 1   Back to the Wall (two players)

Take a ready position with your back within a few inches, or centimeters, of a fence or a wall. A partner 12 to 15 feet (about 4 to 5 m) away tosses 10 balls to your forehand, and you return each of them (bump, don't swing) with a volley (figure 4.2). Don't worry about how you are holding the racket at this point. Avoid letting your racket touch the fence or wall when you take the racket back. Develop a pattern of stepping forward with the opposite foot to hit the ball.

Variation

Take a ready position exactly in the middle of an opened fence gate. A partner stands approximately 10 feet (3 m) away and tosses 10 balls head-high. Step forward (out of the gate) to hit a bump volley back to the tosser.

Figure 4.2 Back to the wall.

TO INCREASE DIFFICULTY

- Volley so that your partner can catch the ball with ease.
- Increase the distance between you and your partner.
- Have your partner increase the speed of the tosses.

TO DECREASE DIFFICULTY

- Decrease the distance between you and your partner.
- Have your partner soften the toss, head-high.
- Have your partner toss only to your forehand or only to your backhand.

Success Check

- Take a short and compact back-swing, like a punch.
- Step forward and away from the fence.

Score Your Success

1 point for every successful bump

Your score: ___ out of 10

The Grip

If you are a beginner, use an Eastern forehand grip for forehand shots (figure 4.3) and an Eastern backhand grip for backhand shots (figure 4.4). Advanced beginners and intermediates should learn to hit with a Continental (hammer) grip on forehands and backhands, but allow enough flexibility to make slight adjustments, depending on the situation. For that reason, it's a good idea to grip the racket loosely enough between shots to make changes but tightly enough on contact with the ball so that you don't lose your grip.

Figure 4.3 **FOREHAND VOLLEY**

Preparation

1. Eastern forehand grip for beginners and advanced beginners (Continental grip for intermediate and advanced players)

2. Off hand on racket throat, then out to help maintain balance

3. Racket head at head height with clear vision

4. Knees bent

5. Weight forward on balls of feet

6. Quick shoulder turn

Swing

1. Firm grip, wrist, and arm

2. Racket head at eye level with clear vision

3. Forward step (not across) with opposite foot at approximately 45-degree angle to net

4. Blocking motion with compact swing; racket face slightly open

5. Arm in relaxed, extended position to slightly more extended position

6. Contact made to side and in front of body

Follow-Through

1. Hit by rebounding ball

2. Weight on front foot at finish

3. Recovery for next shot

MISSTEP

Contact is late.

CORRECTION

Shorten your backswing; extend farther in front.

Figure 4.4 **BACKHAND VOLLEY**

Preparation

1. Eastern backhand grip for beginners (Continental grip for advanced beginners, intermediates, and advanced players)

2. Off hand on racket throat

3. Racket head at head height with clear vision

4. Knees bent

5. Weight forward on balls of feet

6. Quick shoulder turn

Swing

1. Firm grip, wrist, and arm

2. Racket head at eye level with clear vision

3. Forward step (not across) with opposite foot at approximately 45-degree angle to net

4. Blocking motion with compact swing; racket face slightly open

5. Arm in bent position to slightly (not fully) extended position

6. Contact made to side and in front of body

Follow-Through

1. Hit by rebounding ball

2. Weight on front foot at finish

3. Recovery for next shot

MISSTEP

The backhand volley has no power.

CORRECTIONS

Move forward as you hit.

Be sure your grip is firm.

Use your inside thumb to stabilize your wrist.

In the Continental (hammer) grip, the wrist is directly on top of the racket handle (figure 4.5). The thumb has to provide more support from the rear because the wrist is not positioned behind the racket. Extend your thumb along the back of the grip so the inside part of the thumb knuckle is in contact, not the flat part of your thumb.

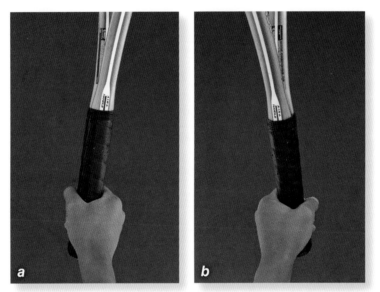

Figure 4.5 Continental grip: *(a)* for a right-handed player; *(b)* for a left-handed player.

On many shots there isn't time to change back and forth between grips. Getting used to an all-purpose grip, however, is difficult and not always appropriate. In such cases, slight adjustments can be made. For example, on a high volley to the forehand side, making a slight wrist movement toward a forehand grip works, as does a move toward a backhand grip on the opposite side. The advantage of the Continental grip is that it prevents having to change grips from the forehand to the backhand. The disadvantage is that some players don't have the forearm strength that the Continental grip requires, or they just never feel comfortable with it.

Volley Drill 2   Hand Behind the Back (two players)

Take a volleying position at the net with a partner at the opposite baseline. Attempt to return 10 shots using the Continental grip. Keep your other hand out of the way to avoid the temptation to change grips and to build strength in your forearm.

TO INCREASE DIFFICULTY
- Place a coin between your racket handle and little finger. If the coin falls out during the preparation, you have changed grips.

TO DECREASE DIFFICULTY
- Hold your free hand at your side to help maintain balance.
- Choke up on the grip.

Success Check
- Use a hammer grip.
- Keep the racket in front of your body, with the racket head up.
- Keep a tight grip on contact.

Score Your Success
1 point for each successful volley return

Your score: ___ out of 10

The Swing

The motion of the volley is more of a punch or a rebound, depending on the pace of the drive hit at you. Your body's forward lean or movement also affects the pace of the ball. Stand in the ready position 8 to 10 feet (about 2 to 3 m) from the net. Move in closer if you are hitting volleys for the first time. Keep the racket directly in front of your body, with your arms extended and your off hand on the racket throat. The racket should be out in front of your body, exactly halfway between your forehand and backhand sides. Keep your weight forward so that your shoe heels barely touch the court. Take a deep bend in the knees to get the feeling of hitting from a crouched position. Bend forward at the waist slightly. Remember, as the ball approaches, you want to be in a position to spring forward.

If the ball comes to your right side, use your right foot to pivot. With your left foot, step forward in the direction in which you want to hit (figure 4.3*b*, the forehand volley swing). Concentrate on moving forward, not to the side. If the ball comes to your left side, pivot on the left foot, and step forward and into the ball with the right foot (figure 4.4*b*, the backhand volley swing). If the ball comes directly at you, slide to one side of the path of the ball by pushing off with one foot and stepping at an angle toward the net with the other. Maneuvering to hit a backhand for these direct shots is easier than maneuvering to hit a forehand.

View your swing for forehand and backhand volleys in a mirror. Remember to look for one component of the swing at a time (footwork, grip, punching motion). If a mirror is not available, close your eyes and visualize the swing.

To be extra alert, many players crouch low and bounce on the balls of their feet when they expect a shot to be hit right at them. If the shot comes low, don't stand straight up and put the racket down to hit the ball. Instead, bend your knees even more and get down to eye level with the ball.

Throughout the entire volley motion, keep your wrist locked so that the racket forms a near 90-degree angle with your forearm. Start the stroke with your arm in a slightly bent position, and extend your arm as you make contact. Do not extend your arm fully; you don't want to make contact with a straight, stiff arm. Lead the stroke with the racket head and dominant hand pushing forward at the same time. Make contact well in front of your body. Attack the ball out in front before it advances on you.

If you have stepped forward, your weight should be on the foot closer to the net. The shoulder closer to the net should be tilted downward slightly. Direct your volleys deep into the backcourt or at an angle to pull the other player off the court.

Use a short follow-through in the direction in which you want to hit, but recover quickly for the next shot. Hit through the ball; do not slow your swing down before making impact. Finish the shot leaning forward with your weight on the front foot.

Volley Drill 3 Forehand and Backhand Volley Setups (two players)

Take a position 8 to 10 feet (about 2 to 3 m) from the net, facing a partner who is close to the net on the opposite side (figure 4.6). Have your partner soft-toss 10 balls alternately to your backhand and forehand sides, higher than eye level. Move laterally toward the net and bump volley the tosses back across the net. Return to the starting position after every hit.

Variation

For variety, have a partner stand about 20 feet (6 m) from you and toss 10 balls to both your forehand and backhand sides. Instead of gripping the racket on the handle, choke up and hold it on the throat for more control. Do not swing hard. Just bump the ball back to the tosser.

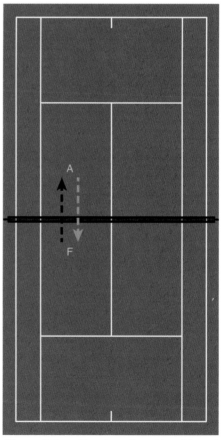

Figure 4.6 Forehand and backhand volley setups.

TO INCREASE DIFFICULTY

- Have your partner toss either right or left randomly.
- Have your partner increase the pace of the toss.
- Have your partner vary the height of the setup.
- Have your partner toss far enough away to make you take more than one or two steps.

TO DECREASE DIFFICULTY

- Have your partner toss only to your forehand side or your backhand side.
- Have your partner stand closer and toss softly, slightly higher than eye level.

Success Check

- Get to the ball in time to hit it at shoulder height.
- Step forward with the left foot on the forehand side and the right foot on the backhand side (for right-handers).

Score Your Success

1 point for each successful bump volley

Your score: ___ out of 10

Volley Drill 4   Consecutive Volleys (two players)

Keep the ball in play by hitting 10 volleys in a row against a partner who rallies with groundstrokes from the baseline (figure 4.7). This drill can be difficult but still fun. Practicing consecutive volleys helps you get used to rapid exchanges. The drill works better if your partner is an intermediate or advanced player. Try to hit volleys deep into the backcourt.

Don't try to win points. Just get used to the idea that not only can you play at the net, but you can also place the ball wherever you want it to go. Later, you can begin hitting volleys with pace and purpose.

TO INCREASE DIFFICULTY

- Volley against two players on the baseline, alternating volleys to each.
- Have the baseline player move inside the service line and exchange consecutive volleys (both players hitting volleys).

TO DECREASE DIFFICULTY

- Move back a step or two from the net to give yourself more time to react.
- Have your partner feed only forehands or only backhands so you don't have to change grips.

(continued)

Volley Drill 4 *(continued)*

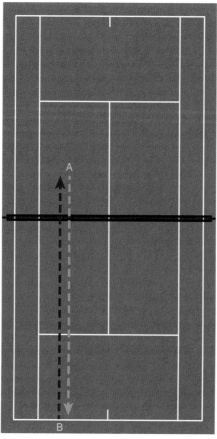

Figure 4.7   Consecutive volleys.

Success Check

- Watch your partner's racket face on contact with the ball.
- Stay light on your feet; keep them moving.
- Recover quickly after each shot.

Score Your Success

1 point for each successful consecutive volley

Your score: ___ out of 10

Low, High, and Wide-Angled Volleys

The face of the racket on a low volley (figure 4.8) will be slightly open because you are bending at the knees instead of at the waist. If the racket face is opened too far, you'll pop the ball up into the air. When you volley up, you allow your opponent to be in a position to hit a winner on the next shot against you. Even if you use perfect technique, the low volley is essentially a defensive shot. Winners are difficult from this position; just get the ball back in play.

For low volleys, aim deep and down the line, or deep and down the middle. When close to the net, practice using underspin to hit a drop volley or no spin to hit a stop volley—one with little or no pace and with backspin. Get low to the ground by bending your knees. Spread your feet to establish a low center of gravity and maintain good balance.

Figure 4.8   Open the racket face on low volleys.

A high volley hit near the net is what every volleyer wants. This type of volley is the way to finish points with crisp, angled shots. If you are inside the service court and your opponent hits a return that fits the description, close in and go for it! Rotate your shoulders early and move your feet quickly, pushing off toward the ball. Use a moderate to short backswing and a short follow-through. Go for a winner into an open corner of the court and recover quickly in anticipation of your opponent's next shot, even if you think the point is over.

The only way to hit an effective wide-angled volley is to move quickly as soon as you anticipate the direction of the ball and see the ball coming. If you are moving parallel to the net, it is difficult to generate any power because your weight is moving to the sideline, not forward. In most cases, your arm has to do more of the work to make up for the lack of forward body movement. Use a compact swing from the shoulder, and lead with the top of the racket head instead of the wrist.

Watch your opponent's racket face to anticipate the direction of his shot. Try to close at an angle toward the net when possible. Consider returning with a crosscourt volley to the side opposite the one from which you are moving. Plant your foot and recover quickly to protect the court you left open.

Volley Drill 5   Target Volleys (two players)

The target volleys drill is designed to help you direct volleys to specific areas of your opponent's court. Use cardboard boxes or ball baskets as targets. Place targets in the forehand and backhand corners. Also place targets short and wide to the right and left sides (figure 4.9). Your partner drops and hits 10 balls to set you up with shots to volley toward each target. Count the number of times you hit the target.

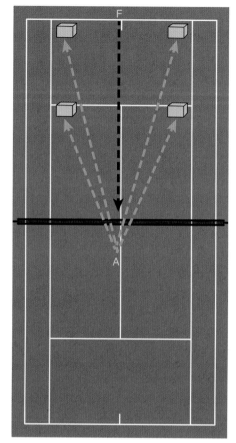

Figure 4.9   Target volleys.

TO INCREASE DIFFICULTY

- Hit forehand and backhand volleys alternately without changing grips.
- Move the targets to different areas.
- Use smaller targets (or tennis ball cans).

TO DECREASE DIFFICULTY

- Have your partner feed only forehand or only backhand shots.
- Use areas of the court as targets instead of boxes.

Success Check

- Make sure your hand and racket move forward together.
- Use a slightly open racket face.
- Aim for an area, leaving room for error.

Score Your Success

1 point for each target hit

Your score: ___ out of 10

Volley Drill 6 **Rapid-Fire Volleys (three players)**

Stand 8 to 10 feet (about 2 to 3 m) from the net in the center of the court (figure 4.10). Two practice partners stand on the opposite baseline, ready to set up two consecutive balls each. The first setter drops and drives two shots in succession toward you (at the net). The setters should never hit harder or faster than you can handle. Return the balls with a volley so they land inside the singles court. As soon as you finish hitting balls 1 and 2, the second setter hits balls 3 and 4. Setters continue hitting rapid-fire feeds for 10 consecutive shots. They do not return the volleys. Count 1 point for each volley successfully returned. Repeat the 10-shot sequence two to five times, depending on how many balls are available.

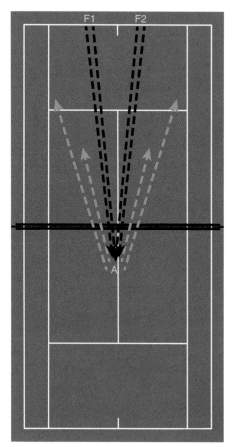

Figure 4.10 Rapid-fire volleys.

TO INCREASE DIFFICULTY
- The setters hit with more pace.
- The setters stand inside the baseline to hit setups.
- Record points only for those volleys that land in the backcourt.

TO DECREASE DIFFICULTY
- The setters feed balls only to your forehand side or your backhand side.
- Count volleys that hit within the singles or doubles sidelines.

Success Check
- Use a Continental grip.
- Keep your weight forward and your racket up.
- Recover quickly.

Score Your Success

1 point for each successful volley

Your score: ___ out of 10

Split Step

Once you have learned how to hit the volley itself, you can work on how to get from the baseline to the net so you can use the stroke. Approaching the net while maintaining good balance requires a move called the split step. The split step will help you spring into action either left or right as your opponent gets ready to strike the ball. To practice the split step, start at the baseline and move forward toward the net. Just before or when you reach the service line, take a short hop to square your feet to the net (figure 4.11). Think of this hop as a hopscotch-type movement you might do on a playground. Without coming to a complete stop, move forward again to hit either a forehand or backhand volley. Timing is important. Execute your split step just a split-second before the other player strikes the ball.

Figure 4.11   Split step.

Volley Drill 7   **Attack (two players)**

Both practice partners exchange groundstrokes from their respective baselines. If either partner hits a weak shot that bounces into the opposite forecourt, the player on that side closes, hitting an approach shot down the line or down the middle. Then she takes the split step on the way to the net for a volley, and the point has begun. Put the ball into play 10 times and keep score. Count the number of points you win.

TO INCREASE DIFFICULTY
- Points are won only by hitting a winning volley (one that is not returned).

TO DECREASE DIFFICULTY
- One partner starts the drill by putting the ball in play with a weak setup.

Success Check

- Hit down-the-line or down-the-middle approach shots.
- Split step after an approach shot as the opponent hits the ball.
- Keep your arms and racket up to make contact in front.

1 point for each point won

Your score: ___ out of 10

Volley Drill 8   Volleys Win (two players)

As a final test, play a set against your practice partner using standard rules, with one exception: either player who wins a point with a volley wins the game. Regardless of the score, the game is won if you or your opponent finishes a point with a volley. Use good judgment when going to the net. Advance to a volleying position because your opponent is in trouble and not because you are going to take a wild chance on winning a game.

TO INCREASE DIFFICULTY

- Replay all points that are not won by a volley, keeping the same score.

TO DECREASE DIFFICULTY

- Play a set in which only one player wins the game by hitting a winning volley.

Success Check

- Hit groundstrokes and approach shots deep to open up volley opportunities.
- Use good judgment when deciding to attack.

Score Your Success

1 point for each game won with a volley

Your score: ___ out of a maximum of 6 games

RETURNING A VOLLEY

Most of the time, you will return your opponent's volleys with groundstrokes from the baseline area. Just as a player hitting volleys has less time to react to your shots, you will have less time to return your opponent's volleys.

The first rule is not to panic. You don't have to hit harder to win the point on the first shot once your opponent has approached the net. Sometimes it takes a setup shot first, followed by a true passing shot (a shot that passes your opponent at the net). Just place the ball where your opponent will have difficulty returning it. You have four return choices:

1. Passing shot to the backhand side

2. Passing shot to the forehand side

3. Jam shot at your opponent's body

4. Lob over your opponent's head

If you can control the ball well enough to return it directly to your opponent, you're good enough to hit it away from the net player.

The second rule is to expect your groundstrokes to be returned quickly. Move into position and get your racket back sooner than you would during baseline exchanges. Don't be surprised at quick returns. Learn to expect them. In tennis, predicting where and how your opponent is going to hit a shot is called anticipation.

Elite tennis players can predict the direction in which opponents will return the ball (some of the time). This skill of anticipation is one of the most valuable assets a player can have. Although reaction time is often perceived to be an inherited characteristic, skilled tennis players use visual information (the ability of an opponent, the type of shot, preparation time, the position of the racket face, the court surface, and the position of the opponent's feet) to react to and anticipate the type, direction, and pace of balls returned to them. Although you may not yet have reached the level of a highly skilled player, it's not too early to begin developing an awareness of the factors that determine where a ball is going.

As the practice partner, you can use volley drills 2, 4, 7, and 8 to practice returning volleys.

SUCCESS SUMMARY

A well-rounded tennis player can use the entire court, including the area at the net. The more you practice volleys, the more comfortable you will be in the forecourt area. Try to develop a variety of volleys—offensive, defensive, high, low, and wide-angled—just as you learned to hit a variety of groundstrokes.

Before beginning your work on the next step, have your practice partner or an instructor check your volley fundamentals. In the absence of an objective observer, go through your own checklist mentally. Remember these basics: short backswing, forward movement, early contact, and firm grip. Allow yourself to be aggressive. When you are in a position to hit volleys, think about attacking, not defending. Try to follow the ball with your eyes all the way to the strings. Even if you think you've hit a winning volley, do not relax. Expect every shot to come back.

For each of the drills in this step, you can earn points to chart your progress. Enter your scores in the following scoring summary, and add them to rate your total success. Your goal is to score at least 38 out of the 76 possible points.

SCORING SUMMARY

VOLLEY DRILLS

1. Back to the wall   _____ out of 10

2. Hand behind the back   _____ out of 10

3. Forehand and backhand volley setups   _____ out of 10

4. Consecutive volleys   _____ out of 10

5. Target volleys   _____ out of 10

6. Rapid-fire volleys   _____ out of 10

7. Attack   _____ out of 10

8. Volleys win   _____ out of 6

Total   **_____ out of 76**

Half Volleys: Getting Out of Trouble

The half volley is a necessary evil—a shot you are forced to hit because you have no other choice. Baseball and softball players sometimes field balls on the short hop. Tennis players have to do the same thing with half volleys, but they do it with a racket instead of a glove.

The half volley is not actually a volley, but rather a forehand or backhand groundstroke hit immediately after the ball bounces on your side of the court. The half volley requires about half the swing used for normal groundstrokes, and you have about half the normal amount of time to prepare for it. When you find yourself in a position in which you have to hit a half volley, it's usually a result of one of the following scenarios:

- You are caught somewhere between the baseline and service line—an uncomfortable position where many shots bounce at your feet.

- You are late moving into position anywhere on the court (for example, trying to get to the net after a serve or approach shot).

- Your opponent has hit a hard drive shot near the baseline before you have had time to move your feet into a position to hit your typical forehand or backhand.

There are only three things you can try to do with the half volley:

1. Return the ball any way you can. Dig it out. The goal is survival, not technique.

2. If time allows, take the chance to actually do something good with your shot. Half-volley the ball as deep as possible into your opponent's backcourt.

3. If your hand reaction time is really good, place your half volley into an open corner of the backcourt, take the offensive, and turn a bad situation into a winning one.

Inexperienced players often find themselves out of position because they don't know where to go. Experienced players know better, yet sometimes they can't do anything about it because they've lost a step or two in court coverage. Even elite players who approach the net following a serve have to hit half volleys when opponents hit great returns at their feet. Doubles players use half volleys often. Regardless of your ability level or age group, keep working on court positioning, but develop the skill required to hit a half volley when you need it. Once you have mastered the half volley, you will have moved from beginner status to an intermediate or advanced level.

HITTING A HALF VOLLEY

Because there is so little time to react for a half volley, there are fewer fundamentals to master. Start with a wide base and a quick sideways turn, or at least turn your shoulders once you determine whether you are hitting a forehand or backhand (figure 5.1). Don't worry about which grip to use. Just hold on firmly to whatever grip you have at the moment so that you won't lose your grip on contact.

MISSTEP
The grip is too loose.

CORRECTION
Hold the racket firmly on contact.

MISSTEP
You are overhitting the ball.

CORRECTION
Block; don't swing.

Figure 5.1   HALF VOLLEY

Preparation

1. Early shoulder turn
2. Wide stance
3. Short, abbreviated backswing

Swing

1. Early contact
2. Firm grip
3. Block ball

Follow-Through

1. Little or no follow-through when returning faster shots
2. Finish stroke when returning slower shots

EXERCISES TO INCREASE GRIP STRENGTH

The volley and half volley require forearm, wrist, and grip endurance and power. Here are four ways to develop both:

1. Squeeze a racquetball or old tennis ball.

2. Perform wrist curls (down) and wrist extensions (up) with lightweight dumbbells.

3. Tie an 8-inch (20 cm) string to the center of a 15-inch (38 cm) broom handle with a 2-pound (1 kg) weight (or lighter) tied to the other end of the string. Roll the string up and then down.

4. Play or practice tennis for progressively longer periods of time.

Of all the strokes in tennis that will test your grip strength, the volley and the half volley rank at the top of the list. You can be in perfect position, you can anticipate what is about to happen, and you can be technically perfect—but if you can't hold the racket tightly enough to keep it from twisting in your hand when you are forced to hit a half volley, you'll probably hit the ball off-center and lose the point. The grip is a component of the player's strength that is usually overlooked, and it can cause problems that keep the player from improving performance. The Exercises to Increase Grip Strength sidebar shows four ways to increase grip strength at home or on the court, using minimal or homemade equipment.

For the half volley, there isn't time to take a big backswing, so don't attempt it. Besides, a long backswing causes you to overhit the ball. All that's needed is to block this shot (returning with a short swing). As you turn your side or shoulders to the net, crouch slightly (as though you are sitting on a bench) while you hit, and stay low throughout the stroke. Get as close as you can to eye level with the ball for balance. Block the ball in front and to the side of your position. Keep your racket head perpendicular to the court. Use your off hand for support on the backhand side to help stabilize the racket.

Don't be concerned about a follow-through on the half volley. Most of the time the follow-through isn't necessary when returning hard-hit shots. Aim your racket face in the direction of a target area, hold tight, and expect something good to happen. On those occasions, however, when you hit half volleys with balls that don't have much pace, the follow-through is relatively normal.

After a half volley, expect the worst and hope for the best. Hit your shot and recover immediately to the ready position, always preparing for the ball to come back. If your opponent returns your shot with a weak setup, take advantage of your good fortune and go for a winner.

Half-Volley Drill 1   **Quick Hits (one player)**

One way to get used to the initial feel of a half volley is the quick hits drill. Stand in the middle of the court a step behind the service line (figure 5.2). Drop and hit 10 shots on your forehand side, trying to make contact as quickly after the ball bounces as possible. Count 1 point for every quick hit that bounces inside the opposite singles court. Listen for the "bang–bang" sound of the ball first hitting the court and then hitting your racket.

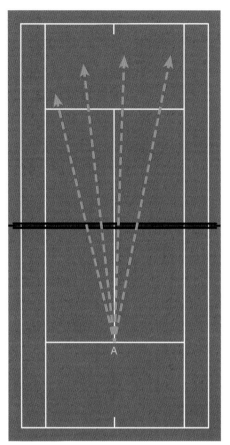

Figure 5.2   Quick hits.

TO INCREASE DIFFICULTY
- Direct shots alternately to the right and left sides of the opposite backcourt.

TO DECREASE DIFFICULTY
- Drop and hit forehands with normal timing, gradually decreasing the time between the bounce of the ball and hitting it.

Success Check
- Maintain a wide stance.
- Keep a firm grip.
- Use a short backswing.

Score Your Success
1 point for every successful shot into the singles court

Your score: ___ out of 10 attempts

Half-Volley Drill 2   Shortstop (two players)

Take a position (without your racket) a few inches or centimeters behind the baseline. Have a drill partner stand at the net on the opposite side and feed 10 balls toward you so that they bounce one to three times. Move into a position in line with the ball, with your knees bent and your hands low to the ground. Field the tennis ball grounders just as a shortstop would field baseballs. Learning to handle tennis balls after they have taken short hops will prepare you for hitting half volleys.

TO INCREASE DIFFICULTY

- Move inside the baseline.
- Have your partner increase the pace of the bounce.

TO DECREASE DIFFICULTY

- Have your partner toss balls rather than hitting them with a racket.
- Have your partner toss balls higher.

Success Check

- Bend more at the knees than at the waist.
- Watch the ball into your hands.

Score Your Success

1 point for every grounder fielded without a bobble

Your score: ___ out of 10 attempts

Half-Volley Drill 3   Rib Ball (one player)

To get a feel for the restricted swinging motion of the half volley, put a ball between the inside of your hitting arm and your ribs (figure 5.3). Now practice half volleys by dropping and putting 10 balls into play. If the ball between your arm and ribs drops, your swing is too long.

Figure 5.3   Rib ball.

TO INCREASE DIFFICULTY
- Keep the ball in play against a partner.
- Count only the shots that hit in the opposite backcourt.

TO DECREASE DIFFICULTY
- Count shots that go over the net.

Success Check

- Use a compact and controlled swing.
- Keep your racket face square to the court surface.

Score Your Success

1 point for every successful shot into the singles court

Your score: ___ out of 10 attempts

Half-Volley Drill 4
No-Man's-Land Rally (two players)

Take a position between the baseline and the service line (figure 5.4). Keep the ball in play with 10 consecutive controlled shots, working as a team with your practice partner, who is in the same position on the opposite side of the net. Restart the drill five times and count the highest number of total "in" shots in each series. Work on control, even on those shots that you have to hit with half volleys. No-man's land is not a good position for match play, but it forces you to practice shots that may help your game later. In this drill, technique is less important than reaction time and quickness.

Variation

A variation of the no-man's-land rally is the quick-time rally. Take a position on the baseline. Keep the ball in play with 10 consecutive shots against a partner positioned very close to the net. Your partner's shots will be returned to you even faster than during the no-man's-land rally. You may have to hit some shots with volleys instead of half volleys. Anticipate where your opponent's next shot will come. Again, technique is less important than reaction time and quickness.

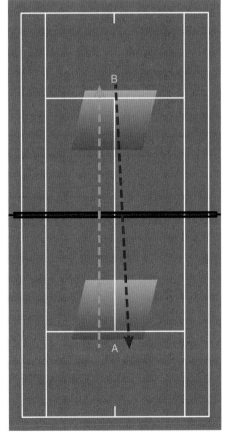

Figure 5.4   No-man's-land rally.

(continued)

Half-Volley Drill 4   *(continued)*

TO INCREASE DIFFICULTY

- Have your partner hit from the baseline.
- Increase the goal to 15 total shots exchanged.

TO DECREASE DIFFICULTY

- Stand deeper in the court, nearer to the baseline.
- Conduct the drill without keeping score.

Success Check

- Bend more at the knees than at the waist.
- Watch the ball hit your strings.
- Use little to no follow-through.

Score Your Success

1 point for each consecutive shot hit between you and your partner

Your score combined with your partner's: ___ out of 10 attempts

Half-Volley Drill 5
Half-Volley Service Returns (two players)

Have a partner practice off-speed serves 10 times while you practice returns from a position one step behind the service line (figure 5.5). Serves have to be "in" to count. Replay faults. Change roles after each round of serves. Along with your half volley, this drill will also improve your service return and reaction time.

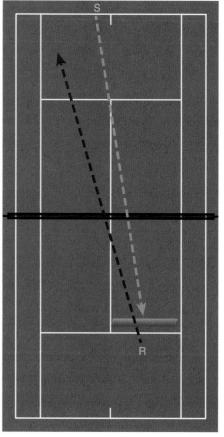

Figure 5.5   Half-volley service returns.

TO INCREASE DIFFICULTY
- Stand on the service line.

TO DECREASE DIFFICULTY
- Stand two or three steps behind the service line.

Success Check

- Use a quick shoulder turn.
- Contact the ball in front.

1 point for each successful service return into the singles court

Your score: ___ out of 10 returns

Half-Volley Drill 6   Hot Seat (four players)

Stand one step behind the service line with a player at the baseline behind you to feed balls (figure 5.6). Two players stand at the net opposite you. The baseline player sets up the volleyers on the opposite side, who hit 10 shots directly at your feet. Dig out as many shots as you can with volleys and half volleys. Count 1 point for each successful return.

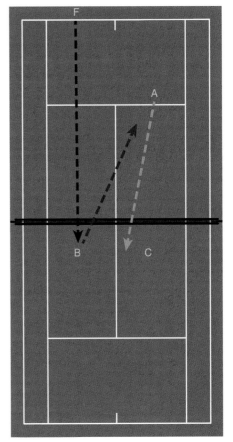

Figure 5.6   Hot seat.

(continued)

Half-Volley Drill 6 *(continued)*

TO INCREASE DIFFICULTY
- Stand on the service line.
- Play the point out.

TO DECREASE DIFFICULTY
- Stand two or three steps behind the service line.
- Conduct the drill against only one player on the opposite side of the net.

Success Check
- Stay in a crouched position.
- Keep your hands and racket forward.
- Use a quick shoulder turn.
- Block; don't swing.

Score Your Success
1 point for each successful return into the singles or doubles court

Your score: ___ out of 10 attempts

SUCCESS SUMMARY

The test of your half-volley technique is whether the ball goes back over the net. The shot doesn't have to look pretty; it just has to be in play. Keep your vision sharp, turn to your side early, and block the ball. Tightly hold the racket and get the racket head low enough to dig the ball out of the court. Scraping the racket head on the court is not anything to be concerned about. The half volley tests your reflexes and fight more than your skill.

Record your score for each of the drills in this step. Enter the scores in the following scoring summary and add your points to rate your total success. Your goal is at least 30 out of 60 points. More is better.

SCORING SUMMARY

HALF-VOLLEY DRILLS

1. Quick hits		_____ out of 10
2. Shortstop		_____ out of 10
3. Rib ball		_____ out of 10
4. No-man's-land rally		_____ out of 10
5. Half-volley service returns		_____ out of 10
6. Hot seat		_____ out of 10
Total		**_____ out of 60**

Lobs: Changing the Pace

New players don't recognize the lob as a weapon. To them, it looks like just another soft, high forehand or backhand. However, players who can use the lob are sure to frustrate those who can't. It is not on a typical list of shots to be practiced, but it should be. A good lob can become an offensive and defensive addition to your growing arsenal of weapons.

If you are a baseline player, you can strategically place a lob over the head of a serve-and-volley player, you can use it to return smashes hit directly at you, and you can hit a lob when you need extra time to recover from a shot that pulls you off the court. If you have trouble with power players, the lob works like a change-up in baseball. It upsets opponents' timing and prevents them from getting into a groove.

There is not much time to prepare for a defensive lob, so the swinging motion is at times little more than an abbreviated block, or rebound, of a ball that has been hit with an overhead smash. Defensive lobs should usually be hit crosscourt to give you more room for error. When you are in control of a point, your preparation for a lob should look as much like a normal groundstroke as possible to prevent an opponent from adjusting to it.

Low, offensive lobs shorten the time your opponent has to react. The shot should be hit in a direction parallel to the closer sideline, just high enough to be out of reach. When possible, lob to the backhand side. Even if your opponent reaches your lob before it bounces, she will have to return it with a high backhand—a very difficult shot for almost all players.

Try a lob occasionally even if you lose the point. If nothing else, it will surprise your opponent. Without the threat of a lob, other players don't have to defend against the possibility. They can anticipate that you are going to keep the ball in play with normal groundstrokes, and that gives them an unnecessary advantage.

Include the lob in your doubles game plan. The alleys are in play after the serve, giving you more space to hit. Returning difficult serves, lobbing on an offensive service return over the player at the net, and lobbing when both opponents are at the net are all ways to set up a winning point. Read step 10 for more about the role of the lob in doubles.

HITTING A LOB

You can hit a lob using either a forehand or a backhand. The grip for a forehand lob (figure 6.1) is the same as that for a forehand groundstroke and can be an Eastern, semi-Western, or Western grip—your choice.

Figure 6.1   **FOREHAND LOB**

Preparation

1. Forehand grip
2. Run and plant foot
3. Short backswing on defensive lobs

Swing

1. Open racket face
2. Low-to-high swing

Follow-Through

1. High racket finish on defensive lobs

2. Complete follow-through on offensive lobs

MISSTEP

Lobs are short and low.

CORRECTION

Aim for the back third of the court, or increase the length of your follow-through.

If you are hitting a defensive lob, you won't have much time to prepare. Making a short blocking motion with a firm grip and keeping your racket face open to lift the ball are about all you can do to stay in the point. If you have more time, swing with a down-to-up motion to get the ball high enough to clear an opponent at the net and deep enough to make him retreat to play the shot.

A backhand lob (figure 6.2) is hit with a backhand grip, which for most people is either a standard Eastern or a modified Western. Players who use a two-handed backhand may have more difficulty hitting a backhand lob because the racket is a little more difficult to maneuver on hard shots hit directly at you. When you have more time to set up for a lob, the motion again is a sweeping down-to-up path of the racket (open face) to lift the ball high and deep.

Figure 6.2 **BACKHAND LOB**

Preparation

1. Backhand grip
2. Run and plant foot
3. Short backswing on defensive lobs

Swing

1. Open racket face
2. Low-to-high swing

Follow-Through

1. High racket finish on defensive lobs
2. Complete follow-through on offensive lobs

MISSTEP

Lobs are hit out.

CORRECTION

Reduce the length of your backswing, don't swing as hard, or compensate for wind at your back.

When you are defending against a smash, you don't have much choice about what to do or how to do it. Staying in the point one more shot is the goal. But when you have time to set up and your opponent is expecting a groundstroke, a well-disguised offensive lob—forehand or backhand—can win the point being played and can give your opponent something else to worry about the next time she comes to the net.

THREE PRACTICE MISTAKES

When was the last time you practiced your lob, your drop shot, or any other shot that is not a particular favorite or strength? Do you ever practice simulated match situations, or do you just wait for them to come along during a real match? Here are three common mistakes players make when practicing and what to do about each one.

1. **Spending too much practice time on strengths.** Baseliners spend hours hitting groundstrokes instead of spending more of that time on serves, volleys, and overheads. Big hitters do just the opposite by practicing their power strokes instead of using that time to become steadier at the baseline. Neither group allocates practice time to specialty shots such as the lob, even though it comes up time after time during a match.

2. **Not practicing match situations.** Most players usually play routine sets or matches when they could be putting themselves in circumstances that frequently occur during competition. For example, it's tough to come back when you are down 15-40 in a game, but it can be done. To prepare for playing from behind, play an entire set during practice starting each game down 15-40. It forces you to become accustomed to that match situation so you won't be facing it for the first time in a real match. You'll be surprised how many times you can come back and win those games.

3. **Being reluctant to play "ugly tennis."** It is understandable to want every match to be a thing of beauty, but it's not realistic. Many matches, especially those against slightly less skilled opponents, are ugly. The better player gets dragged down to a level that is not comfortable and has trouble grinding it out and taking a win, ugly or not. You can't go to practice and deliberately play poorly, but you can make winning points harder. Try playing an entire set in which a point cannot be won until the ball has been in play six shots. The point begins on the seventh shot. This will force you to be patient instead of trying professional, perfect shots to win the point right away.

Hold the racket as you would for any groundstroke, although you may have to hold it tighter just before contact with the ball to withstand the force of an opponent's smash. No special grip is required. If a shot comes to your forehand side, use the grip you have been practicing for forehand groundstrokes. Change to a one-handed or two-handed backhand to hit lobs from the opposite side. Look at it this way: The lob is just another way of executing a forehand or backhand, but it's hit higher, softer, and preferably deeper than a normal groundstroke.

Lob Drill 1   Drop-and-Hit Lobs (one player)

Stand just behind the baseline. Drop a ball to your forehand side and hit a normal groundstroke to your partner, who is positioned 8 to 10 feet (2.4 to 3 m) from the net (figure 6.3). Continue hitting, but each time increase the height and arc of the ball until you are comfortably clearing your partner, who is now extending the racket high above her head. The drill starts when you are ready to hit 10 consecutive lobs. Count the number of times your shot clears the opponent's racket and lands in the backcourt area. If you don't have a practice partner, stand in the parking lot behind a court with a basket of balls. Drop and hit lobs over the fence and into an empty court.

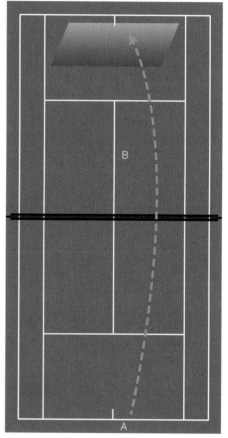

Figure 6.3   Drop-and-hit lobs.

TO INCREASE DIFFICULTY

- Allow your partner to smash any lob hit too low.
- Try the same drill with backhand lobs.

TO DECREASE DIFFICULTY

- Execute the drill without a practice partner.

Success Check

- Use a low-to-high swing path.
- Keep your racket face open.

Score Your Success

1 point for each successful lob into the singles court

Your score: ___ out of 10 attempts

Defensive Lob

In most cases, preparing to hit a defensive lob is a problem. If you are scrambling to survive a point, preparation is seldom the same, and fundamentals take second place to returning the ball high and deep any way you can. Points are not awarded for style. If you have time to set up perfectly with your feet, grip, and backswing, you probably shouldn't be hitting a lob in the first place.

Regardless of the circumstances, consider these techniques when hitting a defensive lob. The first is footwork. Quickly step out and back with the foot on the same side as your dominant arm. Focus on the ball, but turn your shoulders in the direction in which you're moving. Anytime you are in trouble on the court, shorten your backswing. If the other player has hit the ball hard enough, you may be able to just block the ball upward to return it.

Here is one other suggestion to escape from trouble: Direct your lobs crosscourt to reduce the amount of open court to which your opponent can smash. Open your racket face slightly. Lift the ball with a low-to-high swing. Get it well into the air so you'll have enough time to recover and get back into position for the next shot. If you can, follow through to ensure depth on your return. The follow-through will be up and out, away from your body. A full follow-through will help you get the feel of gently lifting the ball into the air and deep into the backcourt. If you make a mistake, it's better to make it too deep or too high rather than too short or too low.

Lob Drill 2   Three-Shot Lob–Smash (two players)

Working against a skilled partner or instructor at the net, stand behind the baseline and put the ball into play 10 times with a lob. Your practice partner hits a controlled smash directed toward your position, which you return with a lob. After each three-shot combination (setup lob, smash, and lob), drop and hit another setup lob. Out of 10 tries, count the number of lobs successfully returned to the singles court following a smash. Intermediate and advanced players often use lob–smash rallies as part of their warm-ups.

TO INCREASE DIFFICULTY
- Keep the ball in play as many times as possible hitting only lobs and controlled smashes.

TO DECREASE DIFFICULTY
- The player at the net hits smashes with less power.
- The player at the net tosses balls deep into the backcourt instead of hitting smashes.

Success Check
- Use a delicate touch.
- Block or deflect the ball; don't swing at it.

Score Your Success
1 point for each successful lob return into the singles court

Your score: ___ out of 10 attempts

Lob Drill 3   Chase It Down (two players)

As you stand on the baseline, have a partner stand at the net and alternately hit 5 set-up shots to your forehand and 5 to your backhand (total of 10)—all driven deep to the corners of the court (figure 6.4). Move to the ball and return shots with lobs. Take short steps to get started; then shift to high gear to run toward the ball. Don't concentrate as much on technique as on chasing the ball and staying in the point for one more shot. If you have a choice, direct your lobs crosscourt.

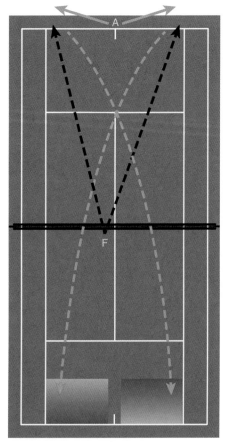

Figure 6.4   Chase it down.

TO INCREASE DIFFICULTY

- Play the point out after the lob; don't take a break before the next sequence.
- Score a point only when your lob lands in the opposite backcourt.

TO DECREASE DIFFICULTY

- Have your partner feed shots only to your forehand corner, and later, only to your backhand corner.

Success Check

- Get a quick start.
- Take the racket back early.
- Aim high, deep, and crosscourt.

Score Your Success

1 point for each successful lob return into the singles court

Your score: ___ out of 10 attempts

Offensive Lob

The offensive lob is designed to win the point by using a shot your opponent doesn't expect. When your opponent expects you to hit a passing shot (a groundstroke that passes him at the net), an offensive lob will catch him off guard, sending the ball over his head for a winner.

Prepare to hit the offensive lob by making it look like any other groundstroke. If you give the preparation a different look, your opponent will anticipate what you are going to do and get into a position to hit a smash. The downside of the offensive lob is that the opportunity to use it presents itself infrequently, and the shot requires more timing and touch than most players are able to master. The offensive lob is not for beginners, but intermediate players can begin to experiment with it.

Advanced players occasionally hit a topspin lob by rapidly brushing the back of the ball with an almost upward motion and the racket face perpendicular to the court. An effective topspin lob clears the opponent's outstretched racket, bounces, and picks up speed as the ball moves away from the hitter and toward the back of the court.

For offensive lobs that don't have exaggerated topspin, open your racket face to direct the ball up. The point of contact may be farther back in relationship to your body than on other shots because you are returning a forcing shot and because waiting another fraction of a second usually means your opponent will be even closer to the net. With an open racket face and a low-to-high swing, lift the ball upward and hit it up to clear your opponent's racket. The ball should be high enough so that your opponent can't reach it before the bounce and deep enough so she cannot return it after the bounce (figure 6.5). If you have a choice, hit to the backhand side.

Follow through in the direction in which you are attempting to hit. The follow-through on the lob may not be as long as it is on other shots, but don't restrict this part of the stroke deliberately. Instead, hold the racket firmly, keep your wrist steady, and try to carry the ball on your strings as long as possible. If you think too much about shortening the follow-through, you may begin to slow down your racket speed before contact.

After a successful offensive lob, follow the line of your shot and move forward to the service line (figure 6.6). If your opponent does get to the ball, he will return it with a lob. If you stay on the baseline, you lose your offensive position. If you go all the way to the net, however, a good lob will put you on the defensive again. From the service line you will have time to move closer to the net for a point-ending smash. If your lob is returned deep into your backcourt, you will still be in position to move back and hit a smash in the air or after the ball has bounced on your side.

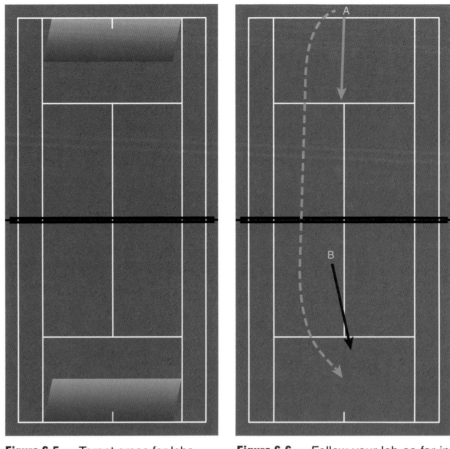

Figure 6.5   Target areas for lobs.

Figure 6.6   Follow your lob as far in as your service line.

Lob Drill 4   **Moonball Rally (two players)**

To practice offensive lobs, take a position on the baseline opposite a practice partner for a moonball rally (figure 6.7). Drop and hit a lob; then keep the ball in play with lobs only. Count the number of combined successful lobs hit into the backcourt. The first shot is a setup lob. Scoring starts on the second shot. Complete the drill three times and count the highest number of "in" lobs out of a maximum of 10.

TO INCREASE DIFFICULTY
- Count only shots that land within 10 feet (3 m, or three steps) of the baseline.

TO DECREASE DIFFICULTY
- Perform the drill in three-shot sequences (setup, lob return, another lob return), and then start again.

Success Check

- Think deep.
- Direct lobs to the backhand side.

Score Your Success

1 point for each successful consecutive lob return by either player into the singles court

Your score: ___ out of 10 attempts

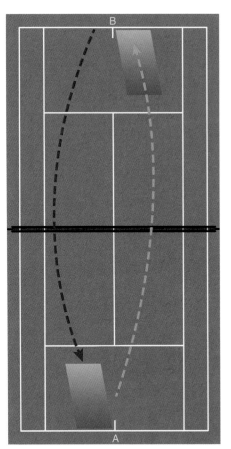

Figure 6.7   Moonball rally.

Lob Drill 5   **Lob Retreat (two players)**

Take a position at the net. Your partner stands at the baseline and lobs 10 balls over your head. Turn and run parallel and to the side of the flight of the ball. Return it with a forehand or backhand lob.

TO INCREASE DIFFICULTY

- Play the point out before continuing the next two-shot sequence.

TO DECREASE DIFFICULTY

- Have your partner hit higher to give you time to reach the ball.

Success Check

- Run to the side of and parallel to the path of the ball.
- Lob high and deep.

Score Your Success

1 point for each successful lob returned into the singles court

Your score: ___ out of 10 attempts

Lob Drill 6   **Lob–Smash Game (two players)**

Stand at the baseline and put the first of 10 lobs into play against an opponent, who begins the game in a forecourt volleying position. Only lobs and smashes are allowed. Remember to follow successful lobs (ones that force your opponent to retreat and hit after the bounce) to the service line. Then be ready to move in even closer for a smash or retreat to retrieve a lob deep into your backcourt.

TO INCREASE DIFFICULTY
- Play the doubles boundaries instead of the singles court.

TO DECREASE DIFFICULTY
- Protect only half the court, from the center mark to the singles sideline.

Success Check
- Block smashes with a firm grip and an open racket face.
- Lob high enough to clear the net player and deep enough to make her retreat.

Score Your Success
1 point for each point won

Your score: ___ out of 10 possible points

RETURNING A LOB

If you are at the net and your opponent tries to lob over your head, you have several options. If you can let the ball bounce without losing your offensive position, play the shot after it has bounced and return the lob with a smash. If you are very close to the net, move in and put the ball away with a smash before it bounces.

If by letting the ball bounce you lose your attacking position, play the ball with a controlled smash while it is in the air. You may not end the point, but you will have put your opponent in a defensive position from which one more shot will finish the point. If you are in a comfortable position, go for a winning shot, either short and angled to pull your opponent wide or deep to keep him in trouble. If you are not set up comfortably, return the lob into your opponent's backcourt with a controlled smash.

If you cannot hit the ball on the bounce or while it is in the air for a smash, turn immediately and sprint in the direction of the ball toward the baseline. Don't run directly under the ball. You have to be able to hit the ball with something resembling a forehand or backhand when you arrive, so move in a line parallel and to the side (typically the forehand side) of the path of the ball and then past it. If you are timing your run to arrive at the same time as the ball, contact will be too late. Think of outrunning the ball to give yourself time to set up. It will make you less rushed when contacting the ball and give you room to swing. If and when you catch up to the lob, return it with your own lob as high and deep as you can. Remember, technique is not as important as staying in the point and giving yourself another chance to win it.

When you are in the backcourt and your opponent lobs, you can play the shot one of two ways. First, you can set up and hit a controlled smash into the backcourt. Second, you can return your opponent's lob with a lob of your own. Moonball rallies (lobs versus lobs) happen occasionally, but they're not very pretty and not much fun.

As the practice partner, you can use lob drills 1, 2, 3, and 6 to practice returning lobs.

SUCCESS SUMMARY

For lobs, use the groundstroke grips you have been practicing and shorten your backswing. If you are in trouble, fight to stay alive even if your technique suffers. Winning a match is war, not a beauty contest. Remember: Practice quick feet, keep an open racket face, use a low-to-high swing, and use enough follow-through to get the ball deep.

Enter your scores for each drill in the following scoring summary; then add them up to rate your total success. Your goal is 30 out of 60 possible points.

SCORING SUMMARY

LOB DRILLS

1. Drop-and-hit lobs	_____	out of 10
2. Three-shot lob–smash	_____	out of 10
3. Chase it down	_____	out of 10
4. Moonball rally	_____	out of 10
5. Lob retreat	_____	out of 10
6. Lob–smash game	_____	out of 10
Total	_____	**out of 60**

Overhead Smashes: Hitting the Put-Away

The overhead smash is your closer, your finisher, your ultimate offensive weapon, and it is probably the most exciting shot in tennis. You've already put pressure on your opponent with strong groundstrokes, a high, deep approach shot, a crisp volley, or perhaps a well-timed lob. The only thing your opponent can do now is retreat and return your shot with a weak, short lob. Now you are ready for the kill.

What you do with overhead smashes depends on where you are on the court. If you are inside the service court, go for winners by hitting into the center of the open part of the court and away from your opponent. When your opponent begins to correctly anticipate where you are going to hit and starts to move in that direction, hit your smash in the opposite direction (behind your opponent). When you have enough time to move back and let a higher ball bounce without giving up your attacking position, go for an angled winner or hit deep into the open corner.

At times, your opponent is an easy target—she is close to the net, directly in front of you, and basically helpless. The unwritten rule is to hit away from or at the feet of your opponent—never to cause an injury. In that situation, an experienced player will turn and allow you to finish the point. By not taking a cheap shot at your opponent, you win not only the point, but also that person's respect.

At times you will be forced to use the overhead smash even though you are in a defensive position. In this situation, the idea is to get the ball back, send it as deep as possible, and hit your mental reset button to continue playing the rest of the point.

HITTING AN OVERHEAD SMASH

Remember these three words when you go for the overhead smash: move your feet! The player who digs into a position too early while waiting for a lob to come down will be in trouble. Several things can alter the expected flight path of the ball, including misjudging its trajectory or speed, not taking the wind into account, and not recognizing spin. Take lots of little steps to get into position, get the racket back and behind your head, and shift your weight forward with your follow-through (figure 7.1). When you make contact, your arm should be extended as high as you can reach and slightly in front of your body.

Figure 7.1   **OVERHEAD SMASH**

Preparation

1. Feet staggered like a quarterback setting up to pass, using short, quick steps

2. Early preparation

3. Hips and shoulders sideways to net

4. Racket back early for abbreviated backswing (on lobs that bounce, use a full backswing)

5. Continental grip

6. Opposite hand pointing to ball, which is in front of body

Swing

1. High reach to hit, contacting ball up and in front of body

2. Hips and shoulders rotate

3. Wrist snaps at contact

4. Close to net, go for winner

5. Away from net, go for placement

Follow-Through

1. Swing through shot

2. Racket moves away from body, across, and then down

3. Move closer to net if opponent returns weak shot

MISSTEP
The smash lacks power.

CORRECTION
Make contact in front of your body.

MISSTEP
Smashes go into the net.

CORRECTIONS
Don't let the ball drop too low.

Reach up to hit with your arm extended.

Keep your head and eyes up.

Grip and Ready Position

The grip on the overhead smash must be either an Eastern forehand or a Continental. Beginners and intermediates may hold the racket with a forehand grip, but almost all advanced players use a Continental (hammer) grip (see the section Continental Grip in step 1). The ready position before a smash is the same as the ready position to hit volleys (see Hitting a Volley in step 4).

PRACTICING THE WRIST FLOP

To practice the wrist flop (pronation), stand close enough to the net to touch it with your racket on an overhead smash motion. Start with your racket behind your head. Now swing upward, but just before the imaginary contact point, rotate your wrist outward and snap down so that both side edges of your racket frame hit the top of the net at the same time. In other words, slap the net with your racket face. If you do it correctly, you should hear a smacking sound on contact. If this is too hard on your wrist, choke up on the throat of the racket until you feel more comfortable with the wrist action.

Backswing and Swing

Once you've recognized that a lob is coming toward you, take the racket back to a position behind your head. Do not take a full backswing. Instead, take the racket back as if you were combing your hair from front to back while turning your body sideways to the net. By shortening the backswing, you won't have to rush your swing toward the ball as it drops, and the motion will reduce the timing margin of error. If you have a good court position, you can still generate enough power to put the ball away or hit to an open area.

As you are taking your racket back, try pointing to the ball with your nondominant hand. This motion may not feel natural at first, but it ensures an early shoulder turn. It may take some time to develop the technique. Pointing can improve your concentration and make you aware of your position in relation to the ball. Use the pointing technique only if it helps you hit better smashes. Pointing is not an essential fundamental for this stroke.

The overhead smash swing motion is similar to a forceful punch serve. Swing your racket upward and forward as if throwing it over the net. Reach as high and outward as you can to make contact. As you swing, shift your weight forward. Hit the ball at an imaginary spot in front of your body.

Because the Continental grip is between the backhand and forehand grip, and because you hit the smash on the forehand side of your body, you have to make some adjustments. Turn your body enough so that your nondominant shoulder is pointing toward the net.

Rotate your wrist outward just before contact. Looking at the back of your hand, your thumb will move away from your body, across, and down. The pronation of the wrist allows you to hit the ball flat and with put-away pace. If you don't flop your wrist, the shot will have too much spin and not enough velocity. However, there are times when smashes should be hit with spin to make the ball curve away and out of the reach of an opponent.

Follow-Through

Make your follow-through out, down, and slightly across your body. Bring the racket through the stroke and return it to the ready position for the next shot. Be aggressive with the smash, but don't assume it's a going to be a winner. It's okay to hit a first smash as a setup and then go for the kill on the second one. Either way, the objective is to finish the point.

Smash Drill 1
Shadow Smash and Touch (one player)

Start at the net, turn to move back quickly (take two or three steps), plant the back foot, and swing through the smash motion without a ball. Then move forward immediately to touch the net with your racket. Complete the series of up-and-back movements 10 times.

TO INCREASE DIFFICULTY
- Retreat more steps after each net touch.
- Increase the number of repetitions from 10 to 15.

TO DECREASE DIFFICULTY
- Execute the drill in slow motion until you feel more comfortable with the routine.
- Reduce the number of repetitions from 10 to 5.

Success Check
- Maintain quick feet.
- Turn sideways to the net when moving back.

Score Your Success
1 point for each shadow smash swing

Your score: ___ out of 10

Smash Drill 2   In or Out (two players)

Sometimes, you don't have to hit a smash because the lob is going out. The more lobs you see, the better feel you'll get for those going in versus those going out. To practice, stand between the net and the service line, ready to hit a smash. Have a partner at the opposite baseline hit 10 consecutive lobs over your head and as close to your baseline as possible. Instead of playing the lob, simply let it go; before it goes over your head, call "In" or "Out." Then turn around quickly to see where the ball lands. Count 1 point for every correct call.

TO INCREASE DIFFICULTY
- Subtract a point for each missed call.

TO DECREASE DIFFICULTY
- Make 5 practice in or out calls before the drill begins.

Success Check
- Read the ball quickly.
- Make mental notes.

Score Your Success
1 point for each correct call

Your score: ___ out of 10

Smash Drill 3
Lob–Smash Combination (two players)

Now you are ready for some live-fire drills. Have a partner or instructor hit short setup lobs from the baseline (figure 7.2). Start the drill from a volleying position, and return 10 lobs directly at the feeder. Reverse roles after each series of lobs and smashes.

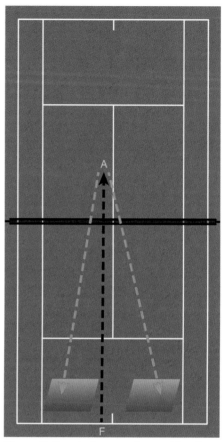

Figure 7.2   Lob–smash combination.

TO INCREASE DIFFICULTY
- Direct your smashes away from the feeder but into the singles court.
- Play the point out after each smash.

TO DECREASE DIFFICULTY
- Stand closer to the net and have your partner hit or underhand toss the lobs lower.

Success Check
- Keep the opposite shoulder toward the net until you are ready to swing.
- Keep your head and eyes up while hitting.

Score Your Success

1 point for each successful smash

Your score: ___ out of 10

Smash Drill 4   Smash to Targets (two players)

Have your practice partner feed 10 lobs from the baseline to you at the net on the opposite side. Return the lobs with smashes directed at large boxes or other targets placed in these positions: deep left corner, deep right corner, right-side service-box corner, and left-side service-box corner (figure 7.3). Choose your target, but count the smash as successful only when a target is hit.

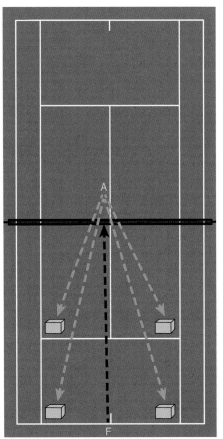

Figure 7.3   Smash to targets.

TO INCREASE DIFFICULTY

- Use smaller targets.
- Direct shots to a different target with each smash.
- Hit targets 1, 2, 3, and 4 in order.

TO DECREASE DIFFICULTY

- Direct shots to the same target with each smash.
- Use larger targets.
- Direct shots to an area of the court instead of at a specific target.
- Reposition the player hitting smashes (up, back, left, or right).
- Reposition the feeder (left or right).

Success Check

- Keep your feet aligned in the direction of the target.
- Focus on control, not power.

Score Your Success

1 point for each target hit

Your score: ___ out of 10

Smash Drill 5
<u>Smash–Volley Combination (two players)</u>

Smashes are often followed by put-away volleys. To practice the smash–volley combination, have a partner stand at the baseline with a basket of balls, ready to feed 10 setup lobs. Start near the net and move into position to smash a setup lob. After each smash, move forward for a winning volley against a short drive setup by your partner with a second ball (figure 7.4). Count 1 point every time you hit both an "in" smash *and* an "in" volley.

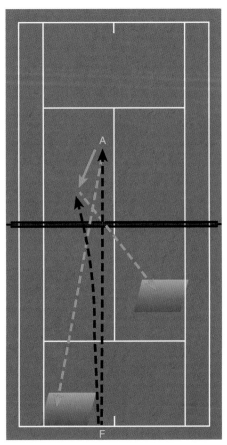

Figure 7.4 Smash–volley combination.

TO INCREASE DIFFICULTY
- Have your partner hit deeper lobs on the first feed and wider setups on the second feed.
- Count combinations as successful only when your volleys are clear winners.

TO DECREASE DIFFICULTY
- Don't keep score; just hit the two required shots.

Success Check
- Recover quickly.
- Keep your arms and racket up and in front for the volley.
- After a smash, immediately move forward, ready to volley.

Score Your Success
1 point for each successful smash–volley combination

Your score: ___ out of 10

Smash Drill 6   **Lob–Smash Game (two players)**

Take a position at the net, and have your partner stand at or slightly behind the baseline. Each point begins with a setup lob hit by your practice partner. Smash the lob, and play the point out. Only the first two shots have to be a lob and a smash, respectively. After the first lob and smash, anything goes. Count the number of points you win out of the 10 points played.

TO INCREASE DIFFICULTY

- Allow your partner to start the point with a deeper lob.
- Earn a point on the third shot if your smash finishes the exchange.

TO DECREASE DIFFICULTY

- Have your partner start the point with a shallow, low lob.
- Score 2 points instead of 1 for every winning smash.

Success Check

- Smash wide to open the court for the next shot.
- Don't smash to the same spot on consecutive shots.

Score Your Success

1 point for each point won

Your score: ___ out of 10

RETURNING AN OVERHEAD SMASH

When you return an overhead smash, reaction time, anticipation, and luck are more important than technique. Forget success checks; concentrate on survival skills. Get the ball in play any way you can. In most cases, this means trying to return the smash with a high, deep defensive lob. Bargain for time and one more chance to stay in the point.

Try to anticipate where the smash will be hit so you can get a head start chasing down the ball. Many players develop a pattern of hitting smashes to the same area of the court. When you observe a pattern of smashes, make a calculated guess as to the direction of your opponent's next shot. Don't stand still and hope the ball comes close. Even if you guess, your chances of guessing correctly are at least 50-50, which may also help distract your opponent. If you show no movement, then your opponent is in total control of the situation and his chance of winning the point is even greater.

Hold your racket even tighter than you hold it on volleys. You will have no time for a backswing. Find a way to get to the ball and block it back with the open face of your racket. If you are good enough or lucky enough to return a smash, recover immediately. You may need another shot to finish the point.

If your opponent makes a mistake and hits a smash that can be returned with a groundstroke, don't overreact. Inexperienced players have a tendency to try to blast the ball with a forehand or backhand once they realize they're still in the point and the ball is not coming as fast as anticipated. Take that extra split-second, assess the pace, and go for a passing shot. It is most unsettling to your opponent when you prove that you are never out of the point, even when the odds are supposedly in her favor.

As the practice partner, you can use smash drills 3, 4, 5, and 6 to practice returning smashes.

SUCCESS SUMMARY

Most players enjoy hitting smashes. You can hit the ball hard and finish the point, one way or the other. The key is preparation. Take quick, short steps to move into the best position. Take the racket back early, and keep the ball in front of your body until it's time to close in for contact. No matter how hard your smash is, it may not be a winner. As soon as you hit to the open court, follow the line of your shot toward the net and recover for the possibility of another lob or an attempted passing shot.

Enter your scores for each drill in the following scoring summary and add them to rate your total success. Set a minimum goal of 30 points out of a possible 60.

SCORING SUMMARY

SMASH DRILLS

1. Shadow smash and touch   _____ out of 10
2. In or out   _____ out of 10
3. Lob–smash combination   _____ out of 10
4. Smash to targets   _____ out of 10
5. Smash–volley combination   _____ out of 10
6. Lob–smash game   _____ out of 10

Total   _____ **out of 60**

Drop Shots: Disguising Your Intentions

The drop shot is basically a forehand or backhand that is hit softly with an open racket face that puts backspin or no spin on the ball. Your shot drops softly over and close to the net, away from your opponent on the other side.

Use the drop shot when you are in a position inside the service line or closer to the net. The idea is to disguise your shot so that it looks as though you are going to hit a forcing shot deep into your opponent's backcourt. Instead, you hit a short drop shot that your opponent can't reach before the ball bounces a second time. Drop shots are usually hit down the line or angled away from the opponent. They are also typically hit after a series of groundstrokes and when the opponent expects a hard, deep, driving shot. The drop shot can be an effective substitute for an approach shot. Although any player can use it, a well-hit drop shot is a relatively sophisticated stroke used by intermediate and advanced players.

The drop shot is especially effective against players who are out of position, out of shape, slow, or uncomfortable at the net (they usually stay back on the baseline during rallies). It also works well against opponents who are hot, tired, or lazy. That's a lot of market potential. If you use the drop shot often enough, your opponent's concern is that you might use it again. This can make other shots from a similar position on the court more effective. The drop shot also forces opposing players out of a backcourt position and their groundstroke-only rhythm of an extended rally.

HITTING A DROP SHOT

The drop shot is all about shot selection, court positioning, and deception. Shot selection means hitting the right shot at the right time—that is, when your opponent is out of position and not expecting a drop shot. Court position is simple. Don't try a drop shot from your baseline. From this position, the drop shot has little to no chance of success. The exception to that rule is that older and highly skilled players may be able to hit drop shots at any time from any position on the court. Deception is the fun part. Hitting a drop shot when your opponent expects something else means you are winning the mental game of tennis as well as the physical game.

Be sure to use drop shots occasionally even if it means losing a point. The drop shot warns your opponent that you have an arsenal of shots and that you are not afraid to use all of them. Just like other strokes and their variations, the drop shot gives you one more option, and for your opponents, one more problem. In tennis, there are great rewards for being deceptive.

Make the drop shot (figure 8.1) look like any other stroke hit from the forecourt. To disguise the shot, don't exaggerate the backswing, delay the stroke, or change footwork. Hold the racket firmly, but not overly tight, and open the racket face or lay the racket face back at the last moment. Some players change to a Continental grip just before they hit to comfortably give the racket face a chance to open up.

Figure 8.1   DROP SHOT

Preparation

1. Forehand or backhand grip
2. Preparation similar to normal ground-stroke

Swing

1. Open racket face
2. High-to-low swing
3. Slower racket-head speed
4. Backspin on ball
5. Ball bounces racket head backward

Follow-Through

1. Abbreviated racket movement after contact
2. Anticipation of next shot

MISSTEP

The shot is too hard, too deep, or too high.

CORRECTION

Open the racket face more, laying the top edge of the racket back, or slow the racket head speed, letting the ball knock the racket head backward.

MISSTEP

Points are lost attempting drop shots.

CORRECTION

Be more patient and selective about when to use the shot, or go back to the practice court for more repetitions.

FIVE STEPS TO INCORPORATING A NEW SKILL

The drop shot definitely falls into the category of a new skill. Unlike with frequently used strokes such as the forehand, backhand, and serve, learning how and when to use the drop shot generally happens later in a tennis player's development.

Incorporating any new skill, including the drop shot, into a sport you already play requires a five-phase progression of learning activities. Professional athletes need several weeks of practice to make a major change. Recreational athletes may need as many as 2,000 repetitions before a new skill becomes second nature.

Step 1: Observation   The first step in learning a new skill is to get a coach, teaching professional, or friend who has the skill to work with you on breaking that skill down into smaller components. Someone who can see only the big picture (e.g., whether a serve goes in or out) is of little help. A skilled observer or teacher can watch for the correct positioning of hands, feet, head, or any other part of the body instead of focusing on the result.

Step 2: Visualization   The second step, visualizing and then shadow-practicing the skill, is skipped by many players but can be a valuable tool in the learning process. It has two parts. First, imagine yourself executing the drop shot. See yourself take the shot in your mind, imagining how you would execute each element of the stroke. You can practice self-visualization on a tennis court, at home, or anytime you have a few moments to see yourself executing the skill.

Second, actually go through the motions by yourself, much like a boxer going through a shadow-boxing sequence or a free-throw shooter going through the motion without a ball before the actual shot. Practicing in this manner takes dedication—you need to be secure enough to tolerate the curious looks that will come when others see you playing an imaginary game. If space permits, try going through the new motion in front of a mirror at home or in a locker room. This scenario is more private and allows you to be your own coach.

Step 3: Simulation   The third step involves working on the new skill by simulating game situations during practice. The soccer player develops a move to get open for a pass. The swimmer makes a perfect turn off the wall. The golfer hits out of a trap and gets close enough to the hole to save par. The tennis player maneuvers an opponent into a position in which a drop shot wins the point. The idea is not to play out the whole game, but instead to repeatedly rehearse the situation in which the new skill will be used.

Step 4: Experimentation   The fourth step is to try the new skill in real but less valuable points, games, matches, or situations. At every level, opportunities exist for experimentation when little or nothing is at stake. You have to be comfortable with the idea that you may hit a terrible drop shot or lose to an inferior opponent because you are taking time to develop a new part of your game.

Step 5: Utilization   The final step is to be confident enough to make the new skill an automatic response in pressure situations. If you have to think about using the drop shot first, it's not ready for prime time. Your readiness is revealed when you no longer analyze, plan, or experiment; you just use it. Like any other tool in your kit, your new drop shot is simply there when you need it.

Start with the racket head above waist level, and swing down behind the ball. Delicately lay the racket face back as if sliding under the ball as you make contact. Slow the speed of your swing. Take a high-to-low swing and open up the racket face more to the sky to give the shot a bit of backspin. Putting backspin on the ball should make it bite into the court surface to slow it down.

Hit the drop shot at the height of the bounce so that the ball falls downward as it clears the net. Slightly clearing the net is effective but not absolutely necessary. Avoid hitting the ball so that it travels too close to your opponent after the bounce. Ideally, the ball should move away from her after the bounce. Never aim for less area than you need to beat your opponent.

Abbreviate your follow-through. The path of the racket will slide down more than forward. Drop volleys (drop shots hit with volleys) are also more effective if the follow-through is not pronounced. Whatever you do, avoid drop shots from a position behind your baseline. Baseline drop shots will give your opponents too much time to recognize the shot and allow them time to get to the ball.

Expect the other player to get to the ball and return it. If it isn't returned, you win the point. If it is, you should be near the net and ready to volley the next shot for a winner. Hitting drop shots on consecutive points may be a good idea. The other player may have to run hard to reach the ball on the first drop shot, and his momentum does not allow for a quick change of direction. A second drop shot hit to the opposite area of your opponent's forecourt could produce a winner.

Drop-Shot Drill 1
Drop-and-Hit Drop Shots (one player)

Stand where the service line intersects the center service line. Drop 10 consecutive balls and hit them with a forehand drop shot into either service court across the net. Make each shot look like your normal forehand preparation and swing. The shot is successful if the ball bounces twice in the opposite court before crossing the service line.

TO INCREASE DIFFICULTY
- Alternately hit shots to the opposite left and right service courts.
- Attempt half of your drop shots with a backhand.
- Make the ball bounce three times before crossing the service line.
- Make the ball roll before it exits the service court.

TO DECREASE DIFFICULTY
- Have a partner softly toss balls to your forehand side.

Success Check
- Keep an open racket face.
- Use a high-to-low swing.

Score Your Success
1 point for each successful drop shot

Your score: ___ out of 10 attempts

Drop-Shot Drill 2
Bump-Up Volleys (two players)

Stand behind the service line opposite a feeder at the service line on the other side of the net. The feeder drops and hits 10 soft shots to your forehand side. Instead of returning the shot with a forehand groundstroke, hit the ball by bumping it up in the air a few inches or centimeters (to take pace off the shot); then volley the ball across the net. You'll hit the ball twice: once with a bump-up volley to yourself and once with a follow-up volley that goes across the net. Hitting a bump-up volley requires that you take pace off an opponent's shot, which is what you have to do when hitting a drop shot. Count 1 point for each successful bump-up volley out of 10 attempts.

TO INCREASE DIFFICULTY

- Stand closer to the net and hit the bump-up shot before it bounces on your side.
- Have the feeder alternately hit shots to your forehand and backhand sides.
- Bump up with the forehand side of the racket head, and volley back to the feeder with the backhand side of the racket.

TO DECREASE DIFFICULTY

- Have the feeder toss balls instead of hitting them.
- Practice "air dribbles" (consecutive bump-ups) first to get the feel of the ball on the racket head.

Success Check

- "Catch" the ball on your racket strings.
- Keep your racket face slightly open.

Score Your Success

1 point for each successful bump-up volley

Your score: ___ out of 10 attempts

Drop-Shot Drill 3
Drop-Shot Setups (two players)

Stand in the center of the court just behind the service line. Have your partner drop and hit 10 shots from her baseline that bounce softly between you and the net. Return each setup with a forehand drop shot that bounces twice before crossing the opposite service line (figure 8.2).

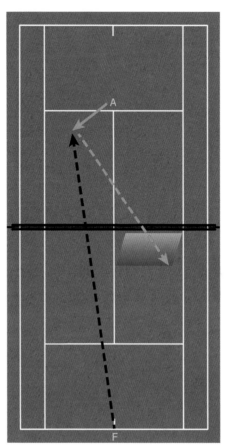

Figure 8.2   Drop-shot setups.

TO INCREASE DIFFICULTY
- Have your partner hit setups randomly to your forehand and backhand sides.

TO DECREASE DIFFICULTY
- Have your partner move forward to the service-line area and hit softer setups.
- Have your partner toss setups instead of hitting them.

Success Check
- Maintain a slow racket-head speed.
- Use noticeable backspin.

Score Your Success
1 point for each successful drop shot

Your score: ___ out of 10 attempts

Drop-Shot Drill 4
Drop-Shot Points (two players)

Stand behind the baseline and have a practice partner stand at the opposite baseline. Your partner drops and hits 10 shots into the forecourt. Move forward, return with a drop shot, and play out the point. Score a point every time you hit the first ball with a drop shot.

TO INCREASE DIFFICULTY

- Allow your partner to start the drill one step in front of the baseline.
- Score a point only if you win the overall point.

TO DECREASE DIFFICULTY

- Change the rules to allow you to hit any shot, including a drop shot, to prevent the baseline player from anticipating the next shot.
- Start the drill from a position behind the service line.

Success Check

- Don't give away your intentions.
- Vary the location of the drop shot, and alternate with a deep volley.

Score Your Success

1 point for each successful drop shot (you don't have to win the point)

Your score: ___ out of 10 attempts

Drop-Shot Drill 5   Short Game (two players)

Both players start at a position just behind the service line. Play a 10-point game against your partner using only drop shots (figure 8.3). Any ball hit hard or that bounces outside the service court is out of play. Put the ball into play with a soft drop-and-hit forehand.

TO INCREASE DIFFICULTY

- One player hits all down-the-line drop shots; the other hits all cross-court drop shots.
- See how close to the net you can bounce your drop shot—less than 20 inches (50 cm) or less than 10 inches (25 cm).

TO DECREASE DIFFICULTY

- Use one service-court area.
- Instead of competing for points, work with your partner to see how many consecutive drop shots you can both hit.

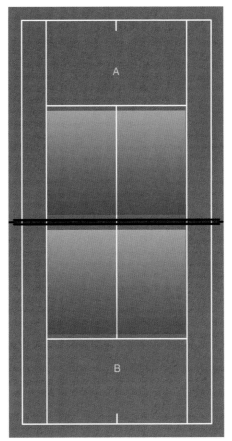

Figure 8.3   Short game.

Success Check

- Recover quickly.
- Use your off hand to adjust your grip.

Score Your Success

1 point for each point won

Your score: ___ out of 10 points

Drop-Shot Drill 6 Drop Shots Win (two players)

Play a set against a practice partner. If either player hits a winning drop shot from the forecourt area, the game is won and over. Regardless of the previous score, the player hitting the drop shot wins the game. Don't try the shot just to win a point or the game. Use the drop shot only when you are positioned near the net and your partner is too far away to get to the ball. Score 1 point for each game won with a drop shot (maximum of 6).

TO INCREASE DIFFICULTY

- Both players must attempt at least one drop shot per game. If not, repeat the game.
- Award a game only when the ball bounces twice on a drop shot before the opponent reaches it.

TO DECREASE DIFFICULTY

- Allow the player hitting the drop shot to use the alleys as well as the service courts as target areas.

Success Check

- Make a quick first step.
- Delay your drop shot until your opponent commits in another direction.

Score Your Success

1 point for each game-winning drop shot

Your score: ___ out of 6

RETURNING A DROP SHOT

Players often give away information on drop shots by not disguising their strokes or by their body language. Observe how your opponent prepares and hits this shot compared to the way he normally hits groundstrokes. You might be able to outguess your opponent and get to the net sooner to hit a winner off his drop shot.

If your opponent is in the forecourt and in a position to hit a variety of shots, you must at least be aware that the drop shot is a possibility. This is especially true if you are well behind the baseline or out wide to either side. Make the other player prove that he can hit this shot before you start looking for it. A successful drop shot by your opponent should not be worrisome unless it becomes a pattern.

As soon as you realize that the drop shot is coming, move toward the ball as fast as you can. If you get there quickly, hit it down the line for a winner. If you have to stretch at the last second, consider returning it over your opponent's head with a lob. Returning a drop shot with a lob is difficult, but the lob may be your best shot because the face of your racket is already open and your forward movement can carry the ball deep. If you attempt the lob and it goes short, turn away and protect yourself.

The third option is a tricky one—returning the drop shot with a drop shot. There are two situations in which a drop-shot return might work, and *might* is the operative word. The first is when your opponent hits a drop shot, anticipates a lob, and starts moving back to cover the court. If your touch is delicate enough to execute the shot, the other player will not be able to recover quickly enough to change direction back toward the net. In the second situation, you can experiment with hitting a sharply-angled drop shot away from an opponent who is close to the net but moving in the wrong direction. If you can pull off this last return option, congratulations. You're well beyond the beginner and intermediate levels—at least on drop shots.

As the practice partner, you can use drop-shot drills 2, 4, and 5 to practice returning drop shots.

SUCCESS SUMMARY

Here is a quick review of drop shot fundamentals: Disguise the shot by making it look as much like your normal forehand or backhand preparation, hit with an open racket face and a high-to-low swing, slow the speed of the racket head, use a delicate touch to put backspin on the ball, and finish with an abbreviated backswing.

In the following scoring summary, enter your score for each of the drop-shot drills. Your goal is 28 out of 56 possible points. If you score higher, you have great touch and can add the drop shot to your collection of weapons.

SCORING SUMMARY

DROP-SHOT DRILLS

1. Drop-and-hit drop shots _____ out of 10
2. Bump-up volleys _____ out of 10
3. Drop-shot setups _____ out of 10
4. Drop-shot points _____ out of 10
5. Short game _____ out of 10
6. Drop shots win _____ out of 6

Total _____ **out of 56**

Singles Tactics: Playing Your Game

The first eight steps have emphasized strokes, not strategy. Now you are ready to use groundstrokes, serves, volleys, half volleys, lobs, smashes, and drop shots in competitive singles situations. The guidelines that follow are not absolute, but they will help you make sound tactical decisions for hitting the most effective shot in most situations. Your opponent, the environment in which you play, your skill level, and an understanding of your own game will have an effect on your singles tactics.

- **Your opponent.** There are certain things you can do against an opponent who clearly has superior skills (see step 11), but tactical planning won't help you win against a player who is simply better—or better than you on the day of the match. At the beginner and advanced beginner levels, focus on what you do well rather than worrying about the ability or patterns of your opponent.

- **Circumstances.** Home-court advantage is as important in tennis as it is in other sports. The type of court surface, the court surroundings, and weather conditions affect players in different ways. If, for example, you have a big (long) backswing when hitting groundstrokes from the baseline, you won't have as much time to prepare when playing on fast or slick courts. If you are a baseline player who hits without a great deal of power, you may play better on slow courts, where the ball bites into the surface, slows down, and sets up for you to hit a manageable groundstroke. Players with big serves and strong volleys prefer fast courts and have an advantage playing on fast surfaces. Players who depend heavily on big serves to win points may not be able to serve as effectively on slow courts because rallies last longer.

  A second example is that local noises are often unnoticed by home-court players but can be distracting to someone not used to them. Third, most players prefer ideal weather conditions, but some are able to use adverse conditions such as strong wind, glaring sunlight, and darker or lighter back-drops to their advantage. Some players play best when the temperature and humidity are high; others, not so well.

- **Your present skill level.** How well can you execute your own shots? If you think you can beat a player by getting to the net and volleying often, but don't have time to practice approach shots and volleys, your game plan is probably not consistent with your skill level—at least not yet. Many former college-level players find it frustrating to make the adjustment from what they were able to do when practicing six days a week to what they can do when playing league tennis one or two days a week. The message here is to have a game plan based on shots you can execute, not on what you used to do or will be able to do when you've had more practice time and experience.

- **Understanding who you are.** Tactical tennis requires more than recognizing your present skill level. It requires an understanding of your game—who you are as a tennis player. After years of experience, you will have become a certain type of player, and that's not a bad thing. Are you a baseline counter-puncher or an aggressive, hard-hitting baseliner? A big hitter only or an all-court player? A risk taker or a scrapper? Are you better at singles, doubles, or mixed doubles? Champions have come from every category on the list, and each player can get better, regardless of style.

When you know who you are and what you are capable of doing, knowledge of singles strategy and tactics will allow you to move to a higher level of performance. You'll be able to use your skills to develop and execute a good game plan—even one that might change during the course of a match. Some people *never* get it! They would rather look good losing (this usually means hitting hard) than look bad winning (playing ugly tennis).

GROUNDSTROKES

In singles, other than the serve, groundstrokes are the basic tools that help you build, or set up, points. Forehands and backhands from the baseline keep the point going, allowing you to apply constant pressure, and put you in a position to hit winners. Good groundstrokes also make opponents hustle, become fatigued, increase errors, and leave part of the court open for future put-away shots. Here are a number of suggestions to make your groundstrokes more effective:

- When returning a serve, stand near the baseline in the middle of the two extreme angles to which the ball can travel after it is served (figure 9.1).

- Return to a position behind the center of the baseline during a groundstroke rally (figure 9.2).

- Bisect the angle of return of all possible shots that your opponent can hit, in the backcourt and at the net. Inside the singles boundaries, imagine how far to your left and right an opponent is likely to hit the next shot, and position yourself in the middle of those two extremes (figure 9.3).

- Return crosscourt groundstrokes with higher, deeper crosscourt groundstrokes.

- During crosscourt exchanges from the baseline, clear the net with room to spare. It's lower in the middle (3 ft, or 0.9 m) than at the singles sideline (3 ft, 6 in, or 1.07 m).

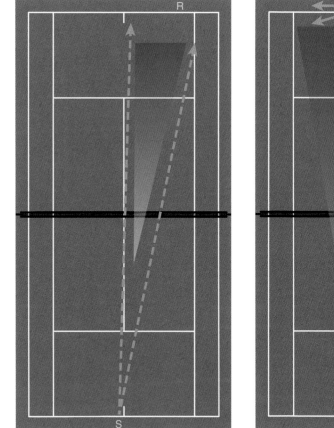

Figure 9.1 Cover the widest possible angles when returning serves.

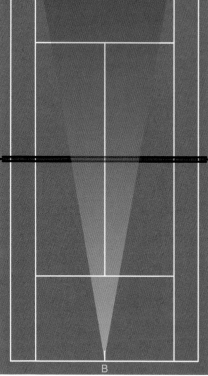

Figure 9.2 Depending on your opponent's position, recover to the center of the baseline between groundstrokes.

- During a baseline rally, develop a pattern and then break it (figure 9.4).

- Move your opponent from corner to corner during baseline rallies. The idea is to play keep-away.

- Hit the ball early after the bounce to gain an offensive advantage. The longer you wait, the more time an opponent has to get into position.

- Use topspin to combine power and control.

- Use topspin on hard passing shots when your opponent is at the net.

- Hit the ball flatter (with little or no topspin) on power groundstrokes.

- Hit topspin groundstrokes higher over the net than you hit flat or slice groundstrokes.

- When hitting a passing shot (to pass an opponent at the net), keep the ball low.

- Don't hesitate on passing shots. Make the decision early.

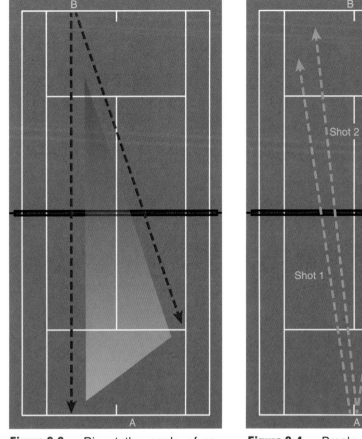

Figure 9.3 Bisect the angle of return of all possible shots.

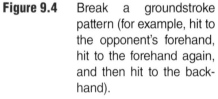

Figure 9.4 Break a groundstroke pattern (for example, hit to the opponent's forehand, hit to the forehand again, and then hit to the backhand).

- Run around your backhand to take advantage of your strong forehand when time permits (figure 9.5; also, see singles tactics drill 1, runaround forehands).

- Run around your backhand and use your forehand to protect against your weak shot.

- Hit approach shots deep and down the line to open up a good angle on your next shot (figure 9.6; also, see singles strategy drill 2, approach-shot setups).

- Hit approach shots down the middle to neutralize an opponent's speed and narrow the angle of the return (figure 9.7).

- Occasionally hit approach shots crosscourt, but only for variety or if you are in a position to put the ball away.

- Hit with an open stance when you are running wide and not in a position to follow your shot to the net.

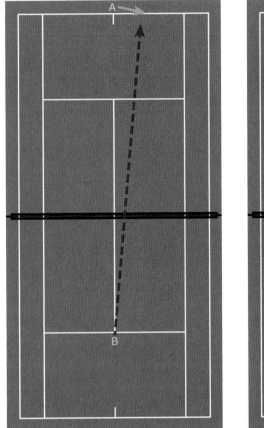

Figure 9.5 Runaround forehands.

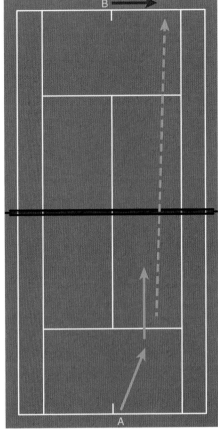

Figure 9.6 Hit approach shots deep down the line to set up a good angle on your next shot.

- Hit with an open stance when footwork time is limited.
- When running wide to retrieve a shot, plant the outside foot when hitting and push off back toward your home base.
- When running wide with no chance to recover for the next shot, go for a down-the-line winner or jam your opponent's body.
- Use a shorter backswing against power players (rebound).
- Use a shorter backswing against a fast serve.
- Slow the pace of a rally with a slice backhand.
- Develop a slice backhand for the return of serve.
- Use a slice backhand return that bounces at the feet of players who rush the net.
- Use a slice backhand to keep the ball low against volleyers.
- Use a slice backhand occasionally on approach shots.

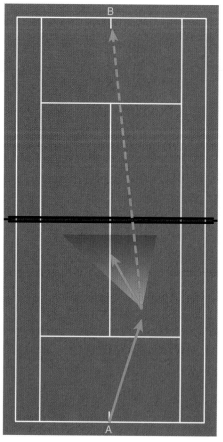
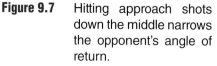

Figure 9.7 Hitting approach shots down the middle narrows the opponent's angle of return.

Singles Tactics Drill 1
Runaround Forehands (two players)

The purpose of this drill is to practice footwork technique while moving quickly to hit a forehand in situations in which you would normally hit a backhand. Begin the drill in the ready position just behind the baseline at the center mark. Have a practice partner stand at the T (where center service line intersects the service line) to feed 10 consecutive balls slightly to your backhand side—some short, some deep (figure 9.8). Run around your backhand and return the setup with a forehand. Recover quickly to your original ready position. Count the number of runaround forehands successfully hit into the opposite singles court.

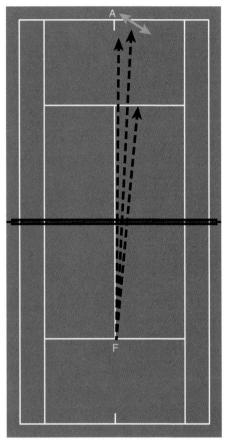

Figure 9.8   Runaround forehands.

TO INCREASE DIFFICULTY

- Count only the shots returned to the singles backcourt.
- The feeder sets shots up wider to the backhand side.
- The feeder sets shots up wide, then center, then wider.
- Award a point only when you hit a clear winner with your forehand (your practice partner helps count).

TO DECREASE DIFFICULTY

- The feeder reduces the pace of setups.
- The feeder sets up shots closer (but not all the way) to the middle of the court.

Success Check

- Maintain quick feet.
- Recover for your next shot.

Score Your Success

1 point for each successful runaround forehand

Your score: ___ out of 10

Singles Tactics Drill 2
Approach-Shot Setups (two players)

To practice placing approach shots down the line, have a partner stand at the baseline and feed 10 consecutive balls short and soft to either forecourt side (figure 9.9). Move forward and hit an approach shot deep and down the line. Count the number of approach shots that fall into a 2 × 2-foot (60 × 60 cm) corner of your opponent's backcourt.

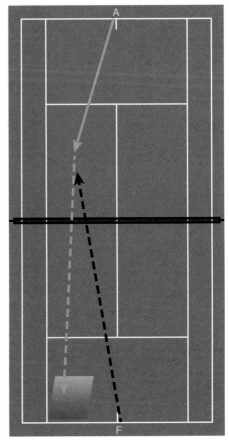

Figure 9.9   Approach-shot setups.

TO INCREASE DIFFICULTY

- Continue playing the point after the approach shot, and score a point only when you win with a volley.

TO DECREASE DIFFICULTY

- Have your partner set up shots only to the forehand or only to the backhand side.
- Have your partner toss instead of hit the setup.

Success Check

- Don't overhit.
- Use a short backswing when moving forward.

Score Your Success

1 point for each successful approach shot

Your score: ___ out of 10

SERVES

On the serve, priority number one is to get the ball in play (see singles strategy drill 3, one serve only). Then you can consider placing the ball while changing pace, location, and spin. If you are not getting at least 60 percent of your first serves in, reduce the pace or add more spin, but completely eliminate the net as your barrier. Make all mistakes deep. Following are ways to get the most out of your serve in singles play:

- Develop a short pre-serve routine.
- Check the receiving (court) position of your opponent before serving to notice any open court area.
- Visualize your target without looking right at it and giving away your intentions.
- Stand near the center mark to serve.
- When serving to a right-hander's backhand in the deuce court, stand close to the center mark.
- If you are right-handed, move a step wider to the right when serving from the deuce court to position yourself to hit a serve that pulls the receiver wide.
- If you are left-handed, move a step wider to the left when serving from the ad court to position yourself to hit a serve that pulls the receiver wide.
- Serve wide with spin to pull an opponent off the court.
- Use spin on the serve for greater control because it clears the net higher.
- Use a spin serve to give yourself more time to get to the net following the serve.
- Serve deep into the service court to keep your opponent from attacking.
- Serve to an opponent's weak side or to an open area.
- Don't attempt aces often. Choose the best times (scorewise).
- When you do attempt aces, think center, where the net is lower and where the distance between you and the inside corner of the service court is shorter.
- Use two medium-paced serves rather than one fast and one slow.
- Serve conservatively when the score is tied or when you are losing late in that game.
- Serve aggressively at 30-0, 40-love, and 40-15.
- Use a variety of serves (pace, spin, and location) during a match.

Singles Tactics Drill 3
One Serve Only (two players)

Play 10 points against a practice partner. You serve to begin every point, but you get only one attempt to get the serve in play (no second-serve attempts). Count the number of times your serve goes in during the 10 points played.

TO INCREASE DIFFICULTY
- Score a point only when you win a point.

TO DECREASE DIFFICULTY
- The server is allowed to serve twice on only 1 point out of the 10 played.
- The server is allowed to serve twice on every other point.

Success Check
- Maintain total focus.
- Serve deep.

Score Your Success
1 point for each "in" serve

Your score: ___ out of 10

Singles Tactics Drill 4   Serve Wide (two players)

If you are right-handed, take a serving position one or two steps to the right of the center mark. Serve 10 balls in a row with sidespin to a practice partner (figure 9.10). If you are left-handed, take a serving position one or two steps to the left of the center mark. Serve 10 balls in a row with sidespin to a practice partner. Score 1 point each time the receiver has to step on or past the singles sideline to return your serve. In this drill, the receiver must begin the point behind the baseline.

TO INCREASE DIFFICULTY
- Serve from a position as close to the center mark as possible.
- Earn a point only by pulling the receiver past the doubles sideline to return your serve.

TO DECREASE DIFFICULTY
- Move three or four steps to the right of the center mark.
- Earn a point every time the receiver has to move toward the singles sideline (instead of going past the singles sideline) to make a return.

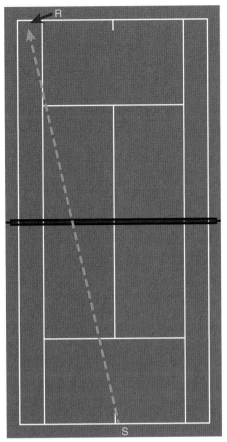

Figure 9.10 Serve wide.

Success Check

- Brush the ball with your racket strings.
- Use rapid racket speed.

Score Your Success

1 point for each successful serve

Your score: ___ out of 10

VOLLEYS

Although it is possible to develop a strong singles game relying almost exclusively on groundstrokes, complete players develop the ability to volley from anywhere on the court. They look for openings to get into volleying positions. They force their opponents into positions where part of the court is left open, and then move in for the kill. Here are many ways to make volleys work to your advantage:

- Take a split step as your opponent gets ready to hit.
- Take a volleying position that bisects the angle of probable returns (figure 9.11).
- Move in closer to the net when you sense that the return won't be a lob.
- Place volleys toward the open part of the court.
- Use a crosscourt volley to return a shot hit down the line (figure 9.12).

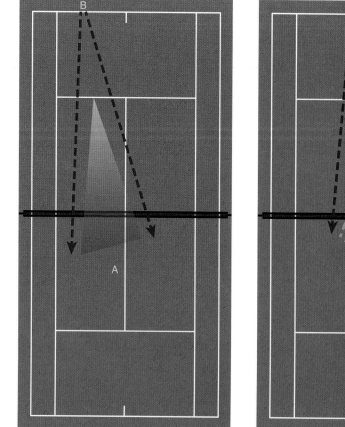

Figure 9.11 Bisect the angle of probable return.

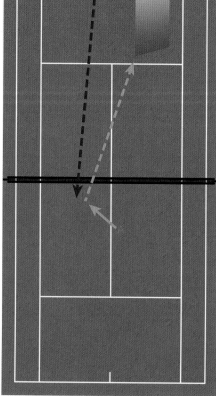

Figure 9.12 Crosscourt volley off a down-the-line passing attempt.

- Use a down-the-line volley to return a shot hit crosscourt (figure 9.13).

- When in doubt, volley deep to your opponent's weaker side or down the middle.

- On low volleys go for safe but deep returns down the line or down the middle.

- On high volleys go for angled winners that bounce inside the service court.

- When you move to hit a volley, try to move forward at an angle toward the net (figure 9.14).

- Use the first volley to set up for a winning second volley.

- After a forcing volley, move closer to the net for the put-away.

- Expect every shot to be returned after every volley.

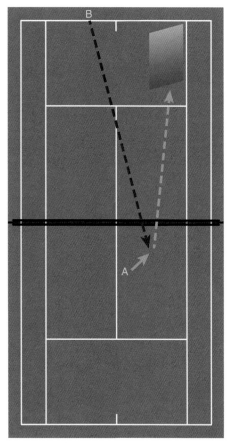

Figure 9.13 Down-the-line volley off a crosscourt passing attempt.

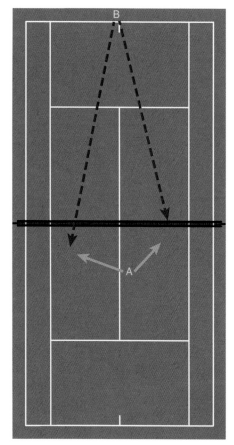

Figure 9.14 Cut off passing attempts by moving at an angle toward the net to hit a volley.

Singles Tactics Drill 5 **Volley–Pass (two players)**

Start in a ready position near the net, and put 10 balls into play so your partner can attempt a passing shot from anywhere on the baseline (figure 9.15). If the attempted passing shot goes shoulder high and down the line, go for the angled crosscourt volley winner. If the ball comes at you low, return it with a volley down the line or down the middle. When the attempted passing shot goes crosscourt, return it with a down-the-line winning volley. Volley–pass is a three-shot drill (setup, passing shot, and volley). Count the number of successfully placed volleys.

TO INCREASE DIFFICULTY

- Play the point out and count only the instances when the volleyer wins.
- Play the point out when an exchange beyond three shots is accomplished, whoever wins.

TO DECREASE DIFFICULTY

- Have the baseline player attempt shots only to the forehand or only to the backhand side.

(continued)

Singles Tactics Drill 5 *(continued)*

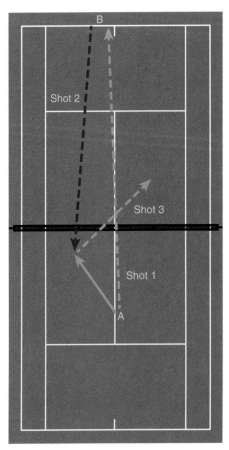

Figure 9.15 Volley–pass.

Success Check

- Stay light on your feet between shots (no idle footwork).
- Keep the racket head up and in front between volleys.

Score Your Success

1 point for each successfully placed volley

Your score: ___ out of 10

Singles Tactics Drill 6
Five-Shot Volley Combo (three players)

Player A begins at the net. Players B and C begin on the opposite baseline. Player A puts 10 consecutive balls into play alternately to players B and C (figure 9.16). Player B hits a down-the-line passing shot, which player A returns crosscourt to player C. Player C keeps the rally going with another down-the-line groundstroke. Player A always hits crosscourt volleys. Players B and C always hit down-the-line groundstrokes. This is a difficult team drill that requires controlled strokes from all three players—not put-away volleys or groundstrokes. When you have completed a five-shot sequence, stop the drill and rotate players to different positions. Count the number of times a five-shot sequence is completed.

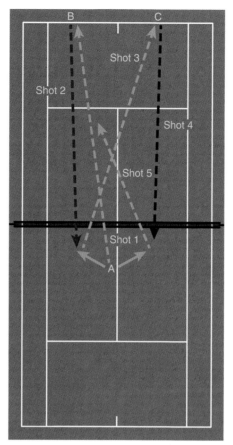

Figure 9.16 Five-shot volley combo.

TO INCREASE DIFFICULTY

- Start over every time an error is made.
- Continue the sequence without stopping after five shots.

TO DECREASE DIFFICULTY

- Pick up the groundstroke–volley sequence from wherever the last error was made.
- Players B and C hit soft groundstrokes; player A hits bump volleys.

Success Check

- Move toward the net (laterally) to cut off passing shots.
- Rebound opponents' groundstrokes.

Score Your Success

1 point for each completed five-shot sequence

Your score: ___ out of 10

LOBS

The lob is especially effective in singles against very aggressive players, hard hitters, and those who have weak smashes. Use the lob often enough to keep your opponent off balance. If it works, use it even more often. Here are some tips for making your lob a successful stroke:

- Hit the lob occasionally just to make your opponent aware that your lob is a threat.

- Lob if your opponent is less mobile, cramping, injured, tired, or old.

- Use the lob more often when your opponent has to look into the sun.

- Lob high to buy time (recover) when you are out of position.

- Lob low with less air time when you are trying to win a point with the shot.

- Hit most defensive lobs crosscourt.

- Follow good offensive lobs to the net. Stop near the service line; then make your next move.

- Lob to the backhand if you have a choice.

- Lob deeper against the wind.

- If you make a mistake with a lob, it's better to make it deep rather than short.

Singles Tactics Drill 7
Approach–Lob (two players)

Begin at the middle of the baseline. Put 10 consecutive balls into play by setting your practice partner up for either a forehand or backhand approach shot, which she hits deep and down the line (figure 9.17). Return the approach shot with a high crosscourt lob. This is a three-shot drill: setup, approach, and lob. Count the number of times a lob clears your opponent at the net, goes crosscourt, and hits between the service line and the baseline.

TO INCREASE DIFFICULTY
- Allow your practice partner to approach the net and smash short lobs.
- Have your practice partner start the drill at midcourt, dropping a ball and driving it deep to the corner.

TO DECREASE DIFFICULTY
- Have your practice partner hit all 10 approach shots to the same corner.
- Score a point for any lob that reaches the backcourt on either side.

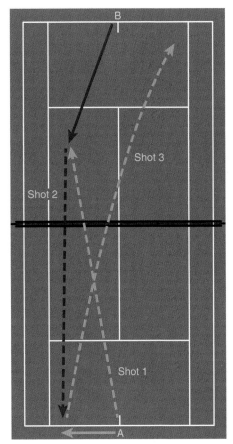

Figure 9.17 Approach–lob.

Success Check

- Use a quick first step.
- Maintain an open racket face.

1 point for each successful crosscourt lob

Your score: ___ out of 10

SMASHES

As you develop into a full-court player, the smash can become the ultimate shot that closes out the point. If you put yourself in a position to win but cannot close the point, your advantage has been wasted. Following are some tips for hitting an effective smash:

- Hit a smash after the bounce if you can do so without losing your offensive position.
- When close to the net, hit smashes flat (without spin) or at an angle (figure 9.18).

- When in the backcourt, use spin to move the ball away from your opponent.

- Do not try a put-away smash when you are near the baseline.

- Hit smashes to a corner when you are deep in your backcourt.

- Change the direction of a second consecutive smash.

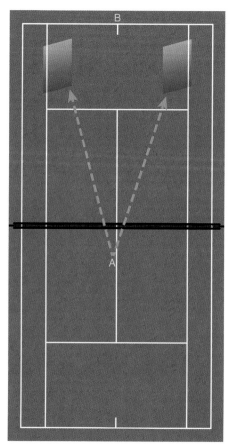

Figure 9.18   Smash at an angle when close to the net.

Singles Tactics Drill 8   **Lob–Smash (two players)**

The lob–smash drill is similar to the approach–lob drill, but with a different kind of pressure setup. Start from the T and hit 10 forcing shots anywhere deep into your opponent's backcourt (figure 9.19). Your practice partner returns the shot with a lob, which you hit with a smash to the open court. Hit three shots—setup, lob, and smash. A successful smash is one that is hit before or after the bounce to the open court.

TO INCREASE DIFFICULTY
- Play the point out, but earn a point only when you win the point with the first smash.
- Start the drill from a position three steps inside the service line.
- Start the drill from a position three steps behind the service line.

TO DECREASE DIFFICULTY
- Play the point out after your smash and earn a point if you win the point in any manner.
- Hit a slower, easier setup for your partner, who hits a lob.

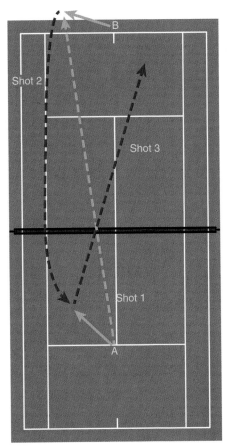

Figure 9.19 Lob–smash.

Success Check

- Maintain quick feet.
- Take the racket back early.
- Point to the ball (that has been lobbed) with your off hand.

1 point for each successful smash

Your score: ___ out of 10

DROP SHOTS

Use the drop shot often enough to keep your opponent honest. Let him know that you can and will try this shot. Don't overuse it, and consider these suggestions regarding drop-shot tactics:

- Use drop shots against slow-moving players.
- Use drop shots against players who don't like to play at the net.
- Use drop shots against players who are in poor physical condition.
- Hit drop shots from the forecourt, not from the baseline.
- Do not try drop shots when a strong wind is at your back.
- Do not try drop shots against players who cover the court well.

Singles Tactics Drill 9
Counter Drop Shot–Lob (two players)

Your practice partner starts at the T and puts 10 balls into play with a drop shot (figure 9.20). You start from the baseline and return your opponent's drop shot with a counter drop shot. Your partner returns your drop shot with a lob, and you both play the point out. Score a point every time you counter your opponent's drop shot with a successful drop shot of your own. A successful drop shot is one that drops softly into the service court and away from your opponent.

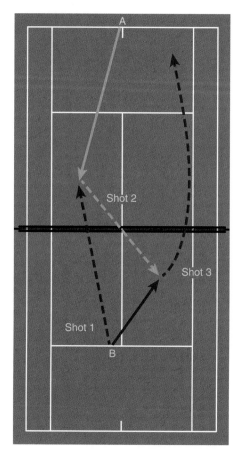

Figure 9.20 Counter drop shot–lob.

TO INCREASE DIFFICULTY
- Both players start from the baseline and rally until an opportunity for a drop shot develops.

TO DECREASE DIFFICULTY
- Both players start from opposing T positions.

Success Check
- Make a quick first step to the ball.
- Use a delicate touch.
- Try to misdirect your opponent.

Score Your Success

1 point for each successful counter drop shot

Your score: ___ out of 10

GENERAL TACTICS

Regardless of the stroke being used in singles play, keep in mind some general tactical guidelines as your game plan evolves. Don't worry about the result. Concentrate on the next shot and the next point. If you find yourself playing "loose" points (those in which you have no particular plan), script the first three shots of each point. Consider these tactics:

- If you win the spin of the racket, choose to serve first if you have a good serve.

- If your opponent chooses to serve first, choose the side against the wind for the first game. Then you'll have two consecutive games with the wind at your back.

- If your opponent chooses to serve first and the wind or sun is not an issue, choose the opposite end from where you warmed up so that the server sees a different view.

- If you are having problems adjusting to a surface, go to the net more often. (Near the net, you can play balls as volleys rather than trying to make groundstroke adjustments after the bounce because of the surface.)

- Slow down the match, within the rules, if you are losing points rapidly.

- When losing with unforced errors, check your stroke fundamentals or change your shot selection before changing your strategy or tactics.

- Hit toward target areas, not lines. Leave a margin for error.

- Use the simplest shot that will win a point. Every shot doesn't have to be great.

- In pressure situations, play the ball and the court, not your opponent.

- Rely on your best shot in crucial situations.

- Anticipate your opponent's best shot in crucial situations.

- Avoid risky shots on critical points (for example, a drop shot from the baseline).

- Periodically, take chances on points you can afford to lose (when you are way ahead in a game or set).

- Don't be afraid to finish the point (see singles tactics drill 10).

Singles Tactics Drill 10
Finish the Point (two players)

Beginners and advanced beginners are often afraid to make mistakes. The result is a "keep-it-in-play" match in which neither player is bold enough to go for a winner—to finish the point. Play 10 points against a practice partner (change servers after every 2 points). If you haven't won the point after hitting six shots during a point, you lose the point. Score 1 point every time you win the point within six or fewer exchanges.

TO INCREASE DIFFICULTY
- You lose the point if you haven't won it within four shots.

TO DECREASE DIFFICULTY
- You lose the point if you haven't won it within seven shots.

Success Check
- Look for an open spot.
- Hit away from your opponent, not to him.

Score Your Success
1 point each time you win a point in six shots or fewer

Your score: ___ out of 10

SUCCESS SUMMARY

Playing styles are not good or bad. They simply either work for you or they don't. Recognize your talents and your limitations on the singles court. Then work hard to become a better player, whatever your style. Enter your score for each of the singles tactics drills in the following scoring summary. If you score 50 out of 100 possible points, you're doing great. Regardless of your score, there is room for improvement.

SCORING SUMMARY

SINGLES TACTICS DRILLS

1. Runaround forehands	_____ out of 10
2. Approach-shot setups	_____ out of 10
3. One serve only	_____ out of 10
4. Serve wide	_____ out of 10
5. Volley–pass	_____ out of 10
6. Five-shot volley combo	_____ out of 10
7. Approach–lob	_____ out of 10
8. Lob–smash	_____ out of 10
9. Counter drop shot–lob	_____ out of 10
10. Finish the point	_____ out of 10
Total	**_____ out of 100**

Doubles Tactics: Playing as a Team

In doubles, court position, anticipation, and shot selection are more important than speed, power, and endurance. Players begin to enjoy doubles and get better at it long after they've achieved success in singles. In some cases, they become better at doubles than at singles, and they can compete at a high level as they get older.

Older players especially enjoy doubles because it's less demanding physically and more demanding mentally. Singles and doubles are both fun to play, but some players prefer individual sports, whereas others like the team aspect. Tennis gives you the opportunity to play both an individual and a team sport.

COURT POSITIONS

Court positions are tactically important both when beginning a point and while it is being played. The most commonly used positions to begin a point are shown in figures 10.1 and 10.2. Both diagrams will be referred to several times in step 10.

- The server (S) serves from a position near a point where the singles sideline intersects the baseline.

- The server's partner (SP) begins the point positioned 8 to 10 feet (2.4 to 3 m) from the net, inside the singles sideline.

- The receiver (R) returns serves from a position approximately where the baseline meets the singles sideline.

- The receiver's partner (RP) stands on the service line between the center service line and the singles sideline. (However, if the receiver is having problems returning serves, the receiver's partner begins the point about halfway between the service line and the baseline or all the way back near the baseline.)

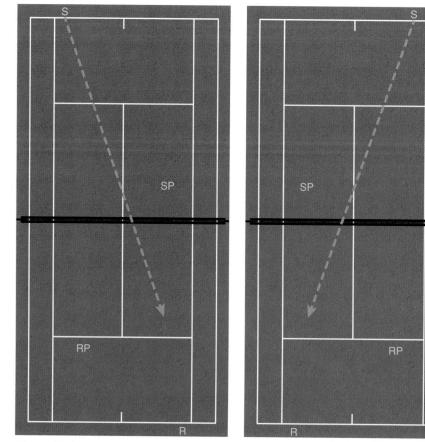

Figure 10.1 Court positions to begin a point in doubles when the server serves from the right (deuce) court.

Figure 10.2 Court positions to begin a point in doubles when the server serves from the left (ad) court.

SERVES

Serving the ball to a specific location sets up the whole point. If you can place your serve, you can control what happens instead of reacting to what your opponents choose to do. Once you determine where the other players are weak or which areas they leave open, you'll need the skill and consistency to hit those spots. The primary objective is to get the ball into play, but putting it in the right places will make things easier for you and your partner. Here are some ways to get the most from your serve:

- Allow the better server to start each set.

- Serve from a position closer to the doubles sideline to place the ball in the service court at an angle that makes a return more difficult.

- Serve deep to the backhand or to an open area.

- Serve down the middle to reduce the angle of return.

- Serve wide to a right-handed player's backhand in the ad (left) court to pull her off the court.

- Serve wide to a left-handed player's backhand in the deuce (right) court to pull him off the court.

- Serve directly at a receiver who has a big backswing.

- Serve down the middle if your partner is good at poaching (moving toward the middle of the court to hit a volley when the receiver returns serve).

- Put more spin on the serve to give yourself time to get to the net.

Doubles Tactics Drill 1
Serve–Rush–Volley (four players)

In this four-person drill, the same person serves 10 points in a row and moves into position to hit a volley from midcourt or closer after the service return (figure 10.3). The receiver returns the ball crosscourt, and the point is played out. Count 1 point for each serve attempt that goes in.

TO INCREASE DIFFICULTY

- Allow a point only when the first serve is in.
- Allow a point only when the server's team wins the point being played.
- Allow a point only when the server is in position to hit a volley after the return of serve.

TO DECREASE DIFFICULTY

- Allow the server two chances to win each point.

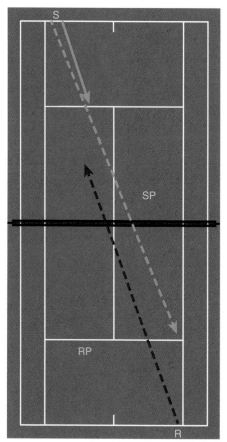

Figure 10.3 Serve–rush–volley.

Success Check

- Serve deep.
- Use a split step before the volley.

Score Your Success

1 point for each successful serve, first or second, that goes in

Your score: ___ out of 10

SERVICE RETURNS AND GROUNDSTROKES

Groundstrokes are necessary, but effective doubles players win with serves, service returns, volleys, and smashes. Forehand and backhand groundstrokes from the baseline are a means of getting into position to win points with volleys and smashes at the net. Consider these tactics:

- Move closer to the service line against players with weak serves.
- If the server remains on the baseline after the serve, return the ball deep and crosscourt; then follow your shot to the net.
- If the server comes to the net after the serve, return the ball crosscourt and to the server's feet (or lob over the server's partner).
- When you try to pass the server's partner at the net, aim for the singles sideline or the middle of the alley.
- Test the server's partner early in a match with a drive or a lob.
- Attempt to pass the server's partner occasionally, even if you lose the point.
- Protect the middle of the court.
- When your partner is forced out of position, shift to cover the middle of the court left open.
- Let the player on your team positioned to hit a forehand take most shots that come down the middle.
- Don't rely on groundstrokes to win in doubles unless your opponents' groundstrokes are erratic.
- When in doubt and your opponents are at the net, hit low and down the middle.
- Force the action to get to the net.

Doubles Tactics Drill 2
Serve–Crosscourt Return (four players)

Play to 10 points. One player serves to the same side (same opponent) each time. The server chooses to stay back after the serve or to move forward to a volley position. If the server stays at the baseline, the receiver sends the ball crosscourt and deep (figure 10.4a). If the server comes to the net, the receiver sends the ball crosscourt but short so that the server has to attempt a low shot (figure 10.4b). No poaching. Continue playing out the point. The player returning serves gets 1 point for each successful return—either deep or short—regardless of who wins the actual point being played.

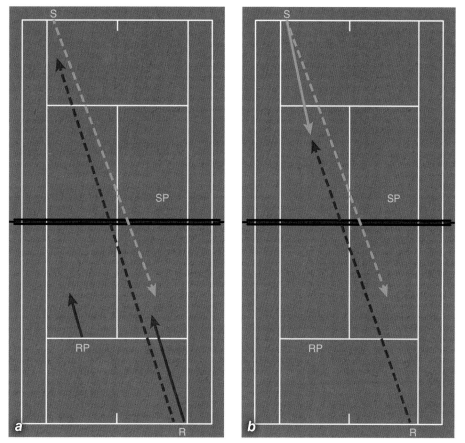

Figure 10.4   Serve–crosscourt return: *(a)* when the server stays at the baseline; *(b)* when the server comes to the net.

(continued)

Doubles Tactics Drill 2   *(continued)*

Variation

Conduct the drill with only two players—the server and the receiver (figure 10.5). After the serve, the server can choose to stay back or follow the serve to a volleying position. The receiver returns the serve and the point is played out, but only crosscourt shots are allowed and only half the court on each side is used.

TO INCREASE DIFFICULTY

- The server's partner may poach (when appropriate) after the serve.

TO DECREASE DIFFICULTY

- The point doesn't begin until the third shot (server serves, receiver returns, server volleys or hits a groundstroke) so that players can get into a rhythm first.
- The server stays back after serving.

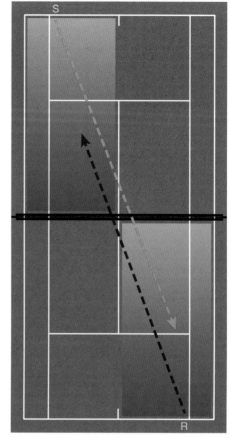

Figure 10.5   Two-player serve–crosscourt return.

Success Check

- Take a short backswing to return serve.
- Return deep if the server stays back; return shallow and low if the server rushes.

Score Your Success

1 point for each successful return of serve

Your score: ___ out of 10

Doubles Tactics Drill 3
Attacking Groundstrokes (four players)

Players A and B play against players C and D (figure 10.6). Teams alternate dropping and hitting the first of 10 shots; then the teams exchange continuous groundstrokes from the baselines. When your opponents hit a short shot into your service court area, move forward together to volleying positions inside the service line. Hit the ball deep and play out the point. Earn 1 point each time you win the point after hitting an attacking groundstroke, advancing to the net, and finishing the point.

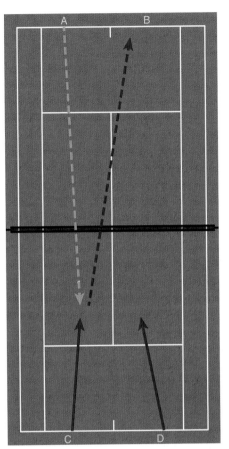

Figure 10.6   Attacking groundstrokes.

TO INCREASE DIFFICULTY
- Keep the ball in play for four shots before the point begins.

TO DECREASE DIFFICULTY
- Designate only one team to attack the net on short shots.

Success Check
- Be aggressive.
- Hit groundstrokes high and deep.

Score Your Success
1 point for each game point won

Your score: ___ out of 10

VOLLEYS AND POACHING

When the server's partner at the net moves across the court to cut off a crosscourt service return with a volley, it's called *poaching*. Poaching is a very effective maneuver for winning points, intimidating the receiver, and keeping the other team off balance. But it is a skill that takes time to perfect in terms of movement, technique, timing, and communication. Poaching has to be used to interject an element of surprise; it should not be something so obvious that the opponents can anticipate what is about to happen.

The movement to poach has to be quick, deliberate, and at an angle toward the net (for power), not parallel to it or in a line away from it (figure 10.7). The technique for the volley used to poach is no different from any other volley. Take little or no backswing, make contact with the ball as early as possible, and go for a winner. If you don't go for a winner, you'll put your team in a difficult court position to win the point. If you are not a strong volleyer, don't poach very often—just enough to pose a threat.

Figure 10.7 Poaching.

Timing is crucial. Make your move at exactly the moment when the receiver has committed to making a crosscourt return. Move too early and you give away the surprise element. Move too late and you can't catch up to the ball.

Communication between partners is the element that requires time to develop. Inexperienced doubles players and those not accustomed to playing with each other should poach rarely—only when they can afford to lose the point.

Some teams use behind-the-back hand signals to indicate an upcoming poach. A closed fist means no poach; an open hand indicates a poach on the next serve. Teams that have played together for a long time don't necessarily need signals. They have a feel for each other in terms of what needs to happen and when it should happen. If you're not sure about whether a poach is the right thing to do in a critical situation, talk to your partner about it before the serve. But sometimes, talking about poaching is *not* an option if you want to keep your opponent guessing.

If you are the server, follow a good serve to the net. If you are receiving the serve, chip the ball short or drive it crosscourt and deep and follow your shot to the net. The team that controls the net usually controls the outcome of the point. That team may not win the point, but it decides who does. However and whenever you approach the net, keep these volleying strategies in mind:

- When your partner serves wide, shift slightly toward the alley.

- When your partner is serving, protect your side of the court, take weak shots down the middle, and smash lobs hit on your side of the court unless your partner calls for the shot.

- When you poach, go for a winner.

- Move diagonally toward the net for a poach instead of parallel to it.

- Poach occasionally, even if you lose the point.

- Poach more often when your partner is serving well.

- Poach more often when your partner serves down the middle than when the serve goes wide.

- Poach less often if your partner is a good serve-and-volleyer.

- Fake the poach at times.

- If you try to poach but can't get to the ball, don't stay in the middle of the court. Get to one side or the other so your partner will know where to go.

- Stand farther from the net if your partner's serve is weak.

- Play farther from the net than usual if you are a stronger player than your partner (to occupy more court space).

- Stand farther from the net against players who lob frequently.

- Play closer to the net against players who seldom lob.

- Watch your opponents, not your partner, when your partner is returning a serve and during rallies.

- During rallies, watch the racket faces of your opponents.

- Shift slightly with every shot to cover the open court.

- When your opponents are set up for a smash, retreat quickly and take a defensive position.

- Change sides and move back to the service line when an opponent lobs over your head.

- In quick exchanges at the net, the last player to hit a shot should take the next shot if it comes down the middle.

Doubles Tactics Drill 4
Serve–Return–Poach (four players)

The server serves 10 times alternately from the right and left sides (deuce and ad courts), and the receiver returns crosscourt each time (figure 10.8). The server's partner poaches when appropriate and volleys to the open court or to the receiver's partner at the opposite service line. Play the point out. Earn 1 point each time you poach and your team wins the point.

TO INCREASE DIFFICULTY
- The server's partner is not required to consistently return in a crosscourt direction.
- Serves must land within 6 feet (1.8 m) of the service line (deep). Mark the court with chalk.

TO DECREASE DIFFICULTY
- Allow the server two attempts on each serve.
- The receiver sets up the poacher with a head-high, medium-paced crosscourt return.

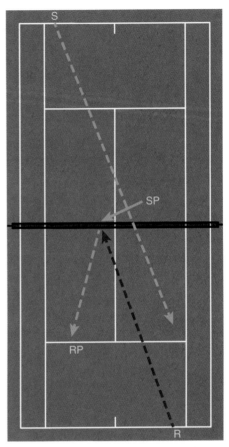

Figure 10.8 Serve–return–poach.

Success Check
- Poach on deep serves.
- Move in a diagonal direction toward the net.

Score Your Success

1 point for each combination of a poach and a point won

Your score: ___ out of 10

Doubles Tactics Drill 5
Continuous Volleys (four players)

Four players are set up in volleying positions, two on each side of the net. Any of the four players puts a ball into play. Players exchange volleys from their positions. After four consecutive volleys, the point is on. Any shot, anywhere, is legal. Score a point each time your team wins the point being played.

TO INCREASE DIFFICULTY
- Earn a point only when a volley you hit wins the point.

TO DECREASE DIFFICULTY
- Begin the point sooner with the second or third setup shot.
- Count the number of consecutive hits by both teams instead of keeping score on points won.

Success Check
- Keep your racket head up.
- Move forward to finish the point.
- Go for the open area on the winner.

Score Your Success
1 point for each game point won

Your score: ___ out of 10

Doubles Tactics Drill 6
Two-Up, Two-Back Volleys (four players)

Players A and B start at the baseline and hit groundstrokes to players C and D, who are volleyers, near the net (figure 10.9). Play 10 points. Either team can put the ball in play. The point begins after the third shot. Once the point is on, both teams try to force a mistake by their opponents. Earn a point each time your team wins the game point.

TO INCREASE DIFFICULTY
- The point begins after the fourth shot.

TO DECREASE DIFFICULTY
- Players on the groundstroke team just keep the ball in play. They cannot hit forcing shots or go for winners.

(continued)

Doubles Tactics Drill 6 *(continued)*

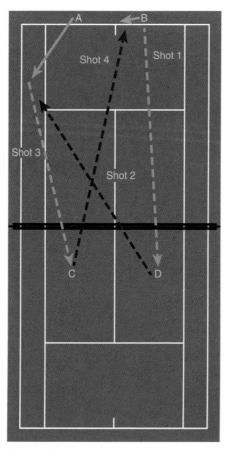

Figure 10.9 Two-up, two-back volleys.

Success Check

- Return low shots with deep, down-the-middle volleys.
- Cut off high shots with angled volleys.
- Protect against the lob.

Score Your Success

1 point for each game point won

Your score: ___ out of 10

LOBS

Although the lob is not a primary weapon in doubles, it should be an integral part of a doubles team's offensive and defensive array of shots. Having a variety of shots and knowing when to use them can offset the power game of aggressive doubles opponents. Following are some tactics to consider:

- Use the offensive lob if the net player poaches often.
- When in doubt, lob deep and down the center of the court.

- Lob low on offense and high on defense.

- Disguise offensive lobs until the last second before contact with the ball.

- Lob over the player who is closer to the net; then follow your lob toward the net.

- Lob over the net player when opponents are playing Australian.

Doubles Tactics Drill 7   Serve–Lob (four players)

Play 10 consecutive points, with the same player serving to the same receiver (figure 10.10). The point starts with the serve. The receiver returns with a lob over the server's partner at the net (who must begin the point 8 to 10 ft, or 2.4 to 3 m, from the net). The net player either smashes the ball back or moves to cover the other side of the court while the server moves to return the lob. The receiver should also follow a successful lob by moving closer for the next shot. Earn 1 point for each lob that clears the server's partner at the net.

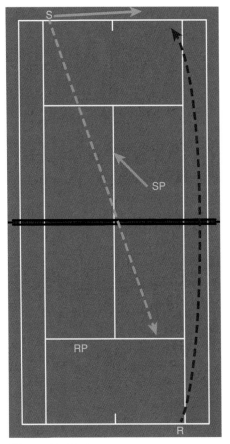

Figure 10.10 Serve–lob.

TO INCREASE DIFFICULTY
- The player at the net sets up farther back to take away open court space.

TO DECREASE DIFFICULTY
- The player at the net starts the point as close to the net as possible, allowing more open court space.
- The receiver has the option of lobbing or returning the serve with a crosscourt groundstroke.

Success Check
- Lob low over the server's partner.
- Move forward and follow the path of the lob.

Score Your Success
1 point for each lob that clears the server's partner

Your score: ___ out of 10

SMASHES

The ability to smash in doubles is essential. If the opponents figure out that neither you nor your partner can hit winning smashes, they will take advantage of the weakness. Because every serving point begins with one player at the net, that person will be tested early to see what happens on a lob to that side. Also, because the idea in doubles is to take away the net from the other team as early as possible, you must be able to finish the point with a winning smash. These tactical guidelines for hitting should help:

- Smash at an angle to open up the opponent's court.

- Smash down the middle to create confusion between your opponents.

- Hit smashes to players out of position.

- Let the partner with the stronger smash take overheads down the middle.

Doubles Tactics Drill 8
Two-Up, Two-Back Smashes (four players)

Play to 10 points. Player A or player B puts 10 balls into play from the baseline using lobs (figure 10.11). At the net, either player C or player D is designated to return the setup lob with a smash. Baseline players move as one unit if the shot is smashed at an angle. Earn 1 point every time the designated player wins the point with a smash.

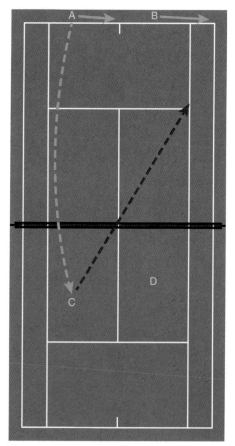

TO INCREASE DIFFICULTY
- Hit setup lobs deeper to start the drill.

TO DECREASE DIFFICULTY
- Hit setup lobs shorter and lower to start the drill.

Figure 10.11 Two-up, two-back smashes.

Success Check

- Make a quick turn and retreat.
- Avoid full-swing smashes.
- Smash down the middle to create confusion.
- Smash wide to open the court.

1 point each time the designated player wins the point with a smash

Your score: ___ out of 10

DROP SHOTS

Using drop shots in doubles is not as easy as in singles and is usually not a good idea. If you try a drop shot, wait until your opponents are far from the net and out of position. Then hit a drop shot to the side of the slower player. If you decide to try a drop shot, do it when safely ahead in a game and a set.

CHOOSING A PARTNER

Whom you play with can be as important as how well you play. Chemistry, compatibility, and complementing each other's games make for successful, long-lasting teams (and friendships). Consider these suggestions when you have a choice of doubles partners:

- Don't assume that a good singles player is a good doubles player.
- Play with someone you like.
- Play with someone who does not criticize you after an error.
- Opposites make good teammates; play with someone whose strengths compensate for your weaknesses. For example, if you are an aggressive, high-strung finisher, find a consistent, calm partner.
- Be more aggressive than normal if your partner is a weaker player. However, accept your role as a team member and don't try to dominate the match.
- Look for a left-handed player–right-handed player combination.
- Play the left-handed player in the ad court and the right-handed player in the deuce court for effective crosscourt returns.
- Play the left-handed player in the deuce court and the right-handed player in the ad court for forehands-down-the-middle coverage.
- Unless you play regularly with the same partner, learn to play the left and right sides when receiving serves.
- Communicate with your partner often.

MIXED DOUBLES

Recreational mixed doubles has some unwritten rules: Everyone has a good time, everyone gets into the action, and everyone comes away from a match in good physical and emotional health.

In tournament competition, these rules do not apply. Competitive mixed doubles should be played similarly to men's doubles and more aggressively than women's doubles. Here are four examples:

- The player with the better serve on the team should serve the first game of each set.

- Serves should be hit with the velocity and to the area in the service court most likely to produce a winning point, regardless of the receiver's gender.

- Shots should be directed to the weaker player unless total control of the match is in hand. Each player should cover his or her side of the court.

- One partner should not cut in front of the other unless percentage tennis (hitting the safest, most effective shot in a given situation) would dictate it.

Choosing positions (left side or right side) in mixed doubles should be determined by two factors: the sides where both players are more effective in returning serves and the sides where both players are more comfortable. Some people believe that the crucial points are played on the ad court and that the stronger partner should play on that side when the other team serves. Even if this theory is true, the advantage of having each player play from the side on which he or she is more effective and comfortable outweighs the crucial point theory.

Because mixed doubles usually has the least priority in practice and playing time, use as many shots as you can to create teamwork problems between opposing players. Moving the ball around the court as much as possible is a good way to manipulate the other team. Lobs are especially effective because one player has to give way to the other, or the partners have to change positions on the court before hitting. Drop shots are usually not a good idea, but they work in mixed doubles to move opponents out of position and open an area for a winning shot.

Finally, make the opposing mixed doubles players do what they don't want to do. If either player is shy about playing the net, make that player come to the net by hitting short shots. If the team is very aggressive and likes coming to the net, use the lob to keep the partners off balance. If one partner wants to dominate, get him out of position. If the partners are not used to playing together, hit a lot of shots down the middle.

SUCCESS SUMMARY

The points in doubles matches begin with very structured shots: Serve to the backhand or to the open court, return crosscourt, approach the net as soon as possible, and force the action. After that, things can get crazy, which is why playing doubles is so much fun. With four players, wider boundaries, and enticing angles, expect wild, long, unpredictable, and exciting points.

Enter your scores for each of the doubles drills in the following scoring summary. The goal is to score at least 40 out of 80 possible points.

SCORING SUMMARY

DOUBLES TACTICS DRILLS

1.	Serve–rush–volley	_____ out of 10
2.	Serve–crosscourt return	_____ out of 10
3.	Attacking groundstrokes	_____ out of 10
4.	Serve–return–poach	_____ out of 10
5.	Continuous volleys	_____ out of 10
6.	Two-up, two-back volleys	_____ out of 10
7.	Serve–lob	_____ out of 10
8.	Two-up, two-back smashes	_____ out of 10
Total		_____ **out of 80**

Special Situations: Managing the Match

From the outside, tennis looks like a very simple sport. Two people (or four people in doubles) hit a ball back and forth over a net until somebody misses. Experienced players, teachers, and coaches know better. In both recreational and competitive tennis, there are situations to be managed and obstacles to overcome.

The first hurdle is to stay focused during a match that can last two hours or longer. Trying to concentrate on anything—reading a book, working on an assignment at school, performing a task—for a long period of time is difficult. Add to that challenge

1. a sport that requires considerable physical and mental skills,
2. fans who are against you,
3. playing surfaces that vary the pace of play,
4. weather conditions that can affect your strokes, and
5. noise that can distract you.

The first part of step 11 addresses concentration. The second part suggests ways to play against various players, personalities, and playing styles. The last section tells you how to adjust to playing conditions such as fast courts, slow courts, wind, hot weather, cold weather, and excessive noise.

Before trying to reach a higher level of concentration, be sure you want to. Millions of players just want to go out, hit the ball, have a good time, and not worry about directing their total focus to the game being played. After all, it's fun to talk with friends, be outdoors, watch others play, and relax. But if you want to play really good tennis, you need to address concentration.

IMPROVING CONCENTRATION SKILLS

Although outside distractions can be a problem, most concentration problems develop from within. We let our thoughts drift. We think about our families, jobs, or studies. We worry about people seeing us make a bad shot. And we think about a thousand other things. Start to improve your concentration skills by reducing as many extraneous thoughts not related to the game as possible, and then work on ways to further sharpen your focus. It is impossible to cut out all nontennis thoughts, but at least try to eliminate the most obvious ones.

Many factors demand your attention during a match. The score in the game or set, the weather, your physical condition, your opponent's condition, and your game plan are all important things to think about. But the time to do that thinking is between points and games, not while the ball is in play.

Your actual play is the most challenging aspect of mental tennis. When the ball is in play, you should focus on two priorities: the ball and the opponent.

The Ball At the top of the list of things to focus on is the tennis ball. "Keep your eye on the ball" should be more than a platitude. If you are serving, try to watch the ball until it leaves your racket strings. If you are receiving the serve, follow the ball with your eyes from the toss, to the point of contact, across the net, and toward your racket. Don't worry about whether the serve is in or out until after you have swung at the ball. There is no penalty for calling a shot out after you hit it. Also concentrate on the ball throughout the point. Watch it when your opponent is preparing to hit and when you are hitting.

Your Opponent As the ball leaves your racket, you will have a second or two to watch where your opponent is on the court and how she is going to hit the next shot. Pay special attention to the other player's racket face before she strikes the ball. You can be faked out of position if you look at anything other than the racket and the ball. Immediately after the ball is hit to you, while focusing on it, also be aware of where your opponent is moving on the court.

Your attention will have to move rapidly back and forth between these two priorities (opponent and ball). Be observant enough to know whether the other player is moving toward the net, returning to the center of the baseline, or moving to one side of the court. Within a split-second, your attention must again return to the ball, but without tunnel vision so that your scope of vision takes in a lot of information.

You'll have an advantage over your opponent if you move into the proper position to execute a stroke automatically rather than having to think about it. Good free-throw shooters in basketball don't think about it; they just shoot the ball. Good hitters in baseball "see the ball and hit the ball." In tennis, you have to prepare for a stroke at the same time you are trying to concentrate on the ball, and you cannot think about both simultaneously. If your strokes have been practiced to the point of thoughtless execution, you can devote full attention to the ball and your opponent.

Focus on Your Game

Try to isolate yourself from the rest of the world for the short period of time you are on the court. Forget for a while that many other things in your life are more important. If you can (and want to), create a temporary attitude in which the next point,

WHAT HAPPENS IN VEGAS

In Las Vegas, a very good tennis player and small-time bettor challenged a professional gambler but mediocre tennis player to a match.

"How much do you want to play for?" asked George, the gambler.

"One hundred dollars a set, two out of three sets," replied Richard, the tournament player.

"No, I won't do that," countered George, "but I'll play you for a thousand dollars a set."

The skilled player was shaken, but he agreed. He lost in straight sets—6-1, 6-2—and the gambler took Richard's $2,000 and went home.

What happened? The better player played not to lose instead of playing to win. It happens in individual and team sports. For a variety of reasons, most of which have nothing to do with money, athletes in positions to win become conservative, tentative, scared, negative, or all of the above.

You can play to win instead of playing not to lose. This step shows you how.

game, or set is more important than your outside stressors. If you set that attitude of pure focus as a goal, any progress toward it should improve your game by sharpening your concentration. Following are seven specific ways to focus or refocus on your tennis game.

Have a Match-Day Routine   Begin with what you do in the morning, including what you eat and how you spend your time up to the minute a match starts. Having a set routine can improve focus tremendously.

Identify Distractions   Awareness of potential problems can help you develop a strategy to cope with them. Make a list. Noise, weather, court surface, and opponents' behaviors or styles are things you cannot control, but you can find a way to overcome them.

Don't Overreact   Rather than overreacting to a problem, find a solution that involves only one or two elements. Come up with some kind of positive cue or change that is simple enough to help you regain focus.

Use Verbal Cues   Spoken and unspoken words or phrases can trigger good performance. Examples are "eyes up" on serves, "hold tight" or "punch the ball" on volleys, and "quick feet" between strokes. For more verbal cues, review the success checks throughout steps 1 to 10.

Reduce Negative Thoughts   Find ways to reduce negative thoughts, and, when possible, turn them into something positive. For example, instead of worrying about the wind, think about how you can use the wind to your advantage. Instead of fretting about a bad call, get mentally ready to win the next point.

Regroup   When things are going badly, slow down. Calm down. Center yourself. Close your eyes. Take a deep breath. Go pick up the third ball or debris on the court. Use the full 25 seconds between points and the 90 seconds during changeovers.

Pull the Trigger (Push Your Start Button)   Do something to direct your attention toward the impending action. Go through the same warm-up routine before a match begins. Bounce the ball a couple of times before a serve. Crouch when anticipating a volley. Bounce (as if taking a split step) between shots.

You will have ups and downs during most matches. Even when you are winning, expect the other player to make a run at you sooner or later. If you are winning, always play as if you are losing and fighting to regain the lead. If you are losing, play the ball and the open court, not the opponent. Check your fundamentals before changing your mental approach. Maintain focus regardless of what happens across the net. The following three drills may help you achieve that goal.

Concentration Drill 1
Silent Practice (two players)

Practice tennis strokes with a partner for 10 minutes without saying a word. Allow nothing to distract you from hitting the ball. Agree ahead of time on a specific practice routine to be followed. Any combination of strokes can be used.

TO INCREASE DIFFICULTY
- Increase the length of silent practice to 15 minutes.
- Play an entire set without talking, except to announce the score.
- Wear earplugs for an entire practice match.

TO DECREASE DIFFICULTY
- Decrease the length of silent practice to 5 minutes.

Success Check
- Do not talk.
- See the ball; then hit the ball.

Score Your Success

1 point for each silent practice minute

Your score: ___ out of 10

Concentration Drill 2
Deuce Games (two players)

Deuce games and tiebreakers are times you must concentrate under pressure. Play 10 games in which every game starts with the score at deuce. Play the ball and the open court, not the point or the other player. If weather conditions are not a factor, change sides after you have completed 5 games.

Variation

Instead of playing 10 points, play three consecutive tiebreakers. Try to stay in the tiebreaker at least 2 more points (extend the tiebreaker). Also, attempt to put 60 percent of your first serves in play while returning 70 percent of your opponent's first serves. To increase difficulty, start each tiebreaker down 1 point or even 2 points. To decrease difficulty, start each tiebreaker up 1 point or even 2 points. Starting with 1 free score-your-success point, earn 3 points for each tiebreaker won.

TO INCREASE DIFFICULTY
- Start each game down 30-40.
- Each player has just one serve rather than a first and second serve opportunity to get the ball in.

TO DECREASE DIFFICULTY
- Start each game at 0-15 or 15-15.

Success Check
- Make each game last at least 4 more points.
- Get first serves in play.

Score Your Success
1 point for each game won

Your score: ___ out of 10

Concentration Drill 3   Five Goals (two players)

Make a list of five goals to be achieved during a set. Earn 2 points for each goal met. Ask a coach or friend to keep track of your goals while you play. Examples of goals include no double faults, winning the first point of each game, coming from behind to win a game, hitting 60 percent of first serves in, hitting 70 percent of service returns in, and winning the set.

TO INCREASE DIFFICULTY
- Increase the number of goals.
- Increase serve and return percentages.
- Increase the number of consecutive points won.

TO DECREASE DIFFICULTY
- Set goals for one game at a time.

Success Check
- Set realistic goals.
- Focus on one goal at a time.

Score Your Success
2 points for each goal met

Your score: ___ out of 10

TEST YOUR CONCENTRATION WITH TRINGLES

Tringles is a format for playing three separate singles matches at the same time on the same court. It is a challenge to concentration because you are playing and keeping score in two matches, while observing a third. The competition (a no-ad set, for example) is between players A and B, players A and C, and players B and C.

Here are the rules:

1. Players A and B each begin the set alternately serving to player C, each from the deuce court and then from the ad court, as in a regular tennis match.

2. After the first point of each game has been played, player A has a score in his game against player C (either 15-0 or 0-15), and player B has a score against player C (also either 15-0 or 0-15).

3. Scores are announced for each separate point by the server as play continues.

4. The player receiving the serve (player C) continues to return serves, playing every point (instead of having to alternate, as players A and B are doing) as long as she wins games.

5. When a server wins a game (player A, for example), he changes places with the person he just defeated (player C). The other server must begin a new game against the new receiver.

6. If you are a server, you have to win a game to change ends of the court and become a receiver. If you are the receiver, you get to keep playing alone as long as you win games.

To decreases difficulty, players keep score only for the games they are playing—not for a set or match.

The Overconfidence Problem

The best player doesn't always win. Judging opponents on the basis of their strokes, record, age, or appearance is a big mistake that often leads to overconfidence. And once the overconfidence train starts rolling, it's hard to stop. Sooner or later, overconfidence meets reality and a correction occurs. The sooner that reality check happens, the less damage there will be.

Self-confidence is a person's (or team's) belief that she (or they) can perform difficult tasks in certain conditions. Overconfidence develops when the person or team misjudges those conditions to a fault. Players tend to pay less attention to detail, ignore critical information, and lack focus before and during a match. All of these factors lead to flaws in judgment that set the stage for losing to an underdog.

Underestimating an Opponent   Overconfidence surfaces in at least two ways, and neither of them is very pretty. The first is to look past a supposedly lesser opponent. An unfocused or a less-than-serious approach to practice is a recipe for disaster, regardless of who the next opponent might be. Preparing for supposedly weaker opponents can be more difficult than getting ready for top-flight competition. It is a perfectly natural response to take for granted a win over players who are smaller, slower, weaker, older, less skilled, or who have a poor record. But it is also possible to lose to a weaker player or team. Underestimation helps weaker players stay in the game.

The athlete or team who underestimates an opponent and gets behind in a contest may have a very difficult time coming back. A lesser competitor or team can be completely outplayed and yet keep the match close, getting lucky or making a great shot near the end to win.

Allowing an Opponent to Hang Around   Allowing the lesser opponent to hang around long enough during a match to gain confidence ties into the risk of overconfidence. Overconfidence breeds carelessness, and it can quickly lead to a reversal in attitudes in which the better player quickly loses momentum and the opponent gains confidence at a faster pace.

In tennis and other sports, there comes a time during the competition when it does not matter who is better on paper. During the last two minutes of a close basketball game, during a sudden-death playoff in golf, or in the last set of a close tennis match, it really doesn't matter who is supposed to be better. Players are more equal at this moment, and it comes down to who makes the play, who gets a break, who is in better condition, or who wants to win the most.

Overconfidence is often the result of athletes being unaccountable for their shortcomings. They think they can bypass a reality check. Those who have exaggerated opinions of themselves—and it happens often among tennis players—look for explanations when things don't work out. They blame coaches, linespersons, teammates, playing conditions, equipment, or whatever they think shifts the blame for underperformance toward someone else. That is one of the reasons some players bounce from coach to coach or partner to partner when things go wrong.

The solution is to prepare, play in the moment, and accept responsibility for your actions. Deal with the situation in front of you. Don't recall the past or believe old news articles about you. Past performance does not guarantee future results.

ADJUSTING TO OPPONENTS

All opponents are not created equal. Some will try to hit the ball hard right at you; others will try to get the ball past you. Some you will enjoy playing against; others you will not. Some are better than you; others are not yet at your skill level. Whatever the case, adjustments can be made to take advantage of your own strengths and of your opponent's weaknesses.

Big Hitters

There are two kinds of big hitters. The first kind hits heavy serves, powerful groundstrokes, put-away volleys, and strong overhead smashes. They like to serve, rush the net, and hit forceful groundstrokes. Their asset is power. Their weaknesses might be a lack of patience, consistency, and sometimes mobility. It is difficult to hit consistently powerful shots for an entire match. Watch for these weaknesses, and be ready to take advantage of them. Most important, don't be intimidated! These big hitters can be beaten, even if they look good while they are losing. Try these tactics against big hitters who like to rush the net:

- Make returning first serves a priority by blocking or rebounding.
- Play a step or two deeper to return serves.
- Play a step closer to challenge the server's concentration.
- Return serves at your opponent's feet when he rushes the net.
- Attack second serves when possible.
- Shorten your backswing when returning power shots.
- Do not fight power with power.
- Slow down the match between points and games.
- Keep the ball deep in your opponent's backcourt.
- Don't panic when you are occasionally overpowered.
- Use the offensive lob, especially early in the match.
- Use two shots—a low, wide drive and then a winner—to pass the player at the net.
- Hit some shots into the body of the power player.
- Try to extend each point beyond four shots.
- Try to extend the match. Balls "fluff up" after lots of big hits, slowing the pace of big hitters.

The second type of big hitter uses power strokes from the baseline, but is not necessarily that good or interested in playing at the net. Against this kind of player, try one or more of these tactics:

- Decide on a quality first shot to take charge of the point.
- Try not to give your opponent her favorite shot.
- Hit short shots occasionally to force her to the net.
- Experiment with hitting serves and groundstrokes directly into your opponent's body.
- Vary the pace, spin, and location of serves.
- As much as possible, dictate the course of the point rather than reacting to what your opponent does.

Adjusting to Opponents Drill 1
Take Your Best Shot (two players)

Play 10 points in which you set up your practice partner with his favorite (can't-miss) finish-the-point shot. Count the number of points out of 10 that you win; then change roles.

TO INCREASE DIFFICULTY

- Allow your opponent to use the doubles alleys.

TO DECREASE DIFFICULTY

- Score a point just for returning the first shot.

Success Check

- Anticipate the direction of the shot.
- Use a quick first step to get to the ball.

Score Your Success

1 point for each game point won

Your score: ___ out of 10

Retrievers (Pushers)

It can be very frustrating to play retrievers—players who get everything back but with little pace. They are certainly not intimidating players, and they probably won't impress you with their strokes. But if you watch these counterpunchers warm up or play against someone else, it is easy to become overconfident.

The problem is that the ball seems to keep coming back no matter how well you play. Players wear themselves out against pushers, spending too much energy and taking too many chances at inopportune times. These retriever-type players know their capabilities, and they play within their limitations. In practice, try the Plan a Point drill. Here are some ideas on how to play these human backboards:

- Make the retriever come to the net.
- Be aggressive when possible.
- Attack the second serve.
- Use wide angles.
- Avoid playing the retriever's style of tennis; he is better at it than you are.
- Stick to your game plan, but play with much patience.
- Respect the retriever as much as any other kind of opponent.
- If you have a choice, avoid playing a retriever on a slow court.
- Anticipate the need to hit extra shots to win the point.
- Plan on long matches.

Adjusting to Opponents Drill 2
Plan a Point (two players)

Play 10 consecutive points and change servers after 5. Plan the first three shots of every point (for example, the first serve will be to the backhand, the second shot will be a crosscourt groundstroke, and the third shot will be a crosscourt winner).

TO INCREASE DIFFICULTY
- Allow your partner to serve every game.
- Score a point only if you win the game.

TO DECREASE DIFFICULTY
- You serve every game.
- Plan only the first two shots of a point.

Success Check
- Focus on your first shot of the exchange.
- Use a variety of plans.

Score Your Success

1 point for each game point won

Your score: ___ out of 10

Left-Handed Players

Left-handed players have an advantage in tennis. The percentage of successful left-handed players seems to be disproportionately high. No one is used to playing left-handers, and few people enjoy the experience. Crucial shots seem to go to the left-handed player's forehand. It can take a whole set or match to figure out their serves. If it makes you feel better, left-handed players also don't like to play against left-handed players. Try these tactics to overcome the left-hander's natural advantages:

- Regroove your strokes to avoid hitting to the left-handed player's forehand side.
- From the right side, serve wide to the left-handed player's backhand.
- Serve down the middle from the ad court.
- Realize that normal put-away shots might go to the left-handed player's strength.

Superior Opponents

Sooner or later, every tennis player has to compete against someone with superior talent. Fortunately, going against someone who is physically superior doesn't have to result in an automatic loss.

Once a match begins, try not to worry about how good your opponent is. You are stuck with each other, so go ahead and play your style of tennis. If you fear that every shot by your opponent will be a winner, you will probably play below your capability. As the match progresses, variables change. Opponents fatigue and balls bounce slower, both of which allow more time for you to get back in the match. Try to relax a little and play each point rather than worrying about the outcome. You may play even better than you normally do. Superior players frequently bring out the best in inferior opponents.

Your opponent is not likely to hit a shot that you haven't seen before. In fact, at some point you have probably returned every type of shot she has to offer. All the other player can do is hit a tennis ball. You might see some shots more often or in different situations, but there aren't that many surprises out there. Try to win points. If you can win a few points, you can win a game. If you can win a few games, you can win a set, and possibly the match.

Following are some specific ways to improve your chances against a player who, at least on paper, appears to be better than you.

Observe   Even elite athletes have weaknesses. Lesser athletes have to look for the few deficiencies that great athletes possess. By observing, making mental notes, or just asking questions, you can accrue points, games, and matches by exploiting minor weaknesses. Maybe it's a weak second serve or perhaps a preference to stay in the backcourt. Perhaps it's a lack of concentration because the focus is on something other than the match.

Work   Physical prowess comes easily to experienced athletes. This doesn't mean that the rest of us can't master sport skills; it just might take longer to reach the same level. Some children learn to read quickly; others require more time and effort. But the result is that both groups can read well. If you can't match your opponent's physical skills, you may be able to make up the deficit by outworking him during practice sessions. Go into the match with the attitude that it will take more than talent to beat you.

Anticipate   Athletes who are a step slower than elite athletes can make up some of the difference in reaction time and speed by anticipating the return. A tennis player starts moving to either the forehand or backhand side in anticipation of where the next shot will be hit. Anticipation is a great equalizer, although it's difficult to quickly acquire the ability and know what is about to happen. This skill takes intelligence, experience, and the physical ability to act on what you have observed. As with every other tennis skill, it comes with time. You have to become a mental statistician.

Control   The worst mistake an underdog can make is trying to play the type of game preferred by the superior player. You can't beat a baseliner by outlasting her on groundstrokes. Shorten points by getting to the net or making her get to the net. Play within your physical limits. One hundred percent of your limited ability may be enough to beat the star who plays at 80 percent perfection.

Survive   Whether it is by skill, guile, luck, or perseverance, your goal is to survive and stay close to the talent-heavy favorite as long as possible. If the score is close near the end of the match, it doesn't matter who has more talent. The person who wins is often the one who makes a big shot, avoids a mental error, is in better physical condition, or just gets lucky. In these situations, physical talent is not a prerequisite; mental strength might be.

Endure   Superior athletic talent does not necessarily carry over from one age group to the next. The person who was physically superior at age 20 may not be the same athlete at ages 30, 40, or 50. Older athletes, in some cases, really are better. The less-than-elite athlete who trains and plays long enough usually emerges as the winner later in life.

When all of the elements needed to be successful in sports are equal, superior talent will win. But things are seldom equal. Sometimes the less-talented tennis player can find ways to win by understanding the little things that super-talented athletes often neglect.

Adjusting to Opponents Drill 3
0-40 Games (two players)

Test your ability to maintain concentration and poise when coming from behind. Play 10 games in which every game is started with the score 40-0 or 0-40 (against you).

TO INCREASE DIFFICULTY
- Allow your opponent to serve every game.

TO DECREASE DIFFICULTY
- Choose to serve or receive serve each game, depending on your strengths.

Success Check
- Return every first serve (get in the point).
- Focus on each point, not the game.

Score Your Success
1 point for each game won

Your score: ___ out of 10

Weaker Opponents

Maintain focus even if you are playing someone you should easily beat. Be nice, but try just as hard to win every point as you would against someone who is your equal or better. If you can win 6-0, do it. Never throw points or games in a match because you feel sorry for the person on the other side of the net. Save your compassion for social tennis. When you are comfortably ahead, work on weak areas of your game, but not at the risk of losing momentum. If an opponent cannot challenge your tennis skills, make the match a challenge to your concentration. Some of the suggestions included in The Overconfidence Problem earlier in this chapter apply to playing against weaker opponents. The handicap scoring drill will help maintain your competitive edge.

Adjusting to Opponents Drill 4
Handicap Scoring (two players)

Play 10 games in which the player losing by one game begins the next game ahead 15-0. If behind by two games, that player begins the next game ahead 30-0. If losing by three or more games, the next game begins at 40-0 (against the winning player).

Variation

Play 10 games (or a set) in which the weaker player is allowed to take three Mulligans. At any point in a set, that player can claim a point without having to play it.

TO INCREASE DIFFICULTY
- The person losing the set gets a choice of serving or receiving every game.

TO DECREASE DIFFICULTY
- The person winning the set never starts a game behind by more than 2 points.

Success Check
- Play aggressively when down in the score.
- Focus on each point, regardless of the score.

Score Your Success
1 point for each game won

Your score: ___ out of 10

Jerks

Some players deliberately try to distract you or interrupt your thinking with an assortment of gamesmanship or unsporting behaviors. Some of the more popular methods are illegally stalling, talking to you or to spectators, arguing, being overly dramatic, and making a bad call just to upset you.

You can handle these situations two ways without totally losing concentration. The first is to decide that nothing an opponent can do will bother you. If you expect trouble from an opponent or even if you get it unexpectedly, make a conscious decision that you will retain your poise and concentration regardless of what happens. Doing so is difficult, and it becomes even more difficult if you are losing. Then, even minor irritations become magnified. It is a lot easier to concentrate when you are winning than when you are losing. Be a good actor.

If peaceful coexistence is not on the agenda, you might as well confront the person and try to solve the problem before the match continues. Don't put up with distractions if worrying about them is going to interfere with your game. If you are thinking about the distractions, you are not thinking about your tennis. Stop the match, call your opponent to the net, and calmly explain what is bothering you. If you don't get any cooperation, ask for an umpire or get a ruling from the tournament referee, if there is one. If the match is merely a social one, do a better job of selecting your opponent next time. Playing this kind of person is not worth the hassle.

Adjusting to Opponents Drill 5
One Free Cheat (two players)

Play 10 no-ad games and allow your opponent to make one deliberately bad call during the set. The "free cheat" may be used at any time, regardless of the score. Your assignment is to retain your poise in spite of being cheated and to continue playing as if nothing unusual happened.

TO INCREASE DIFFICULTY
- Allow your opponent two free cheats per game.

TO DECEASE DIFFICULTY
- Allow both players one free cheat per set.
- Do not allow a free cheat on a game point.

Success Check
- Show no reaction to the bad call.
- Maintain focus.

Score Your Success
1 point for each game won

Your score: ___ out of 10

ADJUSTING TO CONDITIONS

Every opponent is unique, and so is almost every environment in which you play. The type of court, weather conditions, the mood of a crowd, and various distractions will all affect your game and possibly the outcome of the match. The tips in this section will help you adjust to a variety of court speeds, wind conditions, extreme temperatures, and noise, so that every game you play will be a more enjoyable experience.

Court Speed

The casual tennis fan may not know it, but court speed—how the surface of a court affects the bounce of the ball and its velocity after the bounce—determines the outcome of many tennis matches. Many of the great clay-court (slow-surface) players of the world do very poorly on slick, fast courts. And some great fast-court players never win a major title on clay courts. Good tennis players can adjust to any kind of surface, but it takes time. Following are some ways to adjust your game to both fast and slow courts.

FAST COURTS

Playing on a fast, slick court is particularly difficult because the ball skids and stays low after the bounce. The entire pace of the game is faster. Shots seem to be hit harder, rallies are shorter, and less time is available to get into the rhythm of your strokes in the match. If you have to make an adjustment, try to schedule some practice time on the court before match day. Consider these fast-court tactics:

- Turn your shoulders quickly, get the racket back early, and start your swing sooner.
- Rely less on full-body rotation to prepare for groundstrokes.
- Use the open stance as much as needed on groundstrokes.
- Bend your knees and stay low to hit groundstrokes.
- Rely less on topspin and more on flat or slice groundstrokes.
- Play deeper than usual, especially on the serve return.
- Make returning first serves a priority.
- Block fast serves instead of swinging at them.
- Return serves low and at the feet of a net-rushing server.
- Apply less spin on serves to take advantage of the power boosts you'll get on fast surfaces.
- Don't overhit setups. Let the fast court provide extra pace.
- Attack all short balls without overhitting, and hit them behind your opponent.
- Go to the net on medium-deep shots that you would not normally follow.
- Expect your opponent to be more aggressive than on a slow court.
- Expect short rallies.

SLOW COURTS

Adjusting to a slow court is easier than adjusting to a fast court. On slow, rough courts, the ball slows down and bounces higher than it does on fast courts. Instead of having less time to prepare for shots, you will have more than enough time on a slow court. You won't be able to put shots away as easily, and you may become impatient because the points last longer. Retrievers love these courts, and power players detest them. Everyone can win a few more points by trying these slow-court tactics:

- If you are comfortable with them, use Western and semi-Western grips on high-bouncing groundstrokes.
- Use a bigger backswing to generate power.
- Hit with topspin to create high bounces.
- Rely more on serve placement and spin than on power.
- Be selective about when to advance to the net. Your opponent will have more time to hit a shot.
- Do not underestimate the retriever on a slow court.
- Improve your physical stamina.
- Be more deliberate than on fast courts.
- Be patient.
- Expect long rallies.

Wind

There are two ways to deal with the problem of playing in windy conditions. The first is to dread the whole experience, complain about conditions, and blame poor play or losses on windy conditions. The other approach is to try to use the wind to your advantage. When the wind is in your face, it can keep shots in the court that would normally go out. When the wind is at your back, it can add pace to the average or weak shot, and it can cause more trouble for your opponent than for you. The trick is to become so involved in the match that you don't worry about the wind. These strategies will help you deal with windy conditions:

- Choose to warm up and play against the wind in the first game of a match. (You'll change ends after that first game, and then you'll have two consecutive games with the advantage of the wind at your back.)
- Toss the ball lower on the serve.
- Lob less, especially when playing against the wind.
- Set up closer to the net when the wind is against you.
- Hit more aggressively when the wind is against you.
- When the wind is with you, let it help provide some of the power on your strokes, but keep them low.

Extreme Temperatures

It would be nice to play all matches in weather that is 68 °F (20 °C), with 50 percent humidity, but that rarely happens. Serious players have to prepare for competition in an extreme climate as if it were an added opponent. They acclimate themselves to the temperature as much as possible by wearing the proper clothing, consuming the right foods and fluids, and pacing themselves to endure difficult situations. The ones who are successful turn the obstacles of extremely hot and cold weather into assets.

HEAT

Don't ignore the problems hot weather can create. Players who try to prove how tough they are run the risks of cramping, dehydration, fatigue, and not being able to hold onto a sweaty grip during long points. When playing in extremely hot weather, consider these key points:

- Don't wear yourself out trying to hit hard serves, especially on slow courts.
- Make your opponent move around the court—side to side; up and back.
- Conserve energy between points.
- Take the full 90 seconds on changeovers.
- Keep your racket grip dry with towels, wristbands, and drying agents.
- Alternate rackets often enough to keep the grip dry.
- Dress comfortably and coolly with loose-fitting tops.
- Wear light-colored or air-vented apparel that reflects rather than absorbs the heat.

- Drink cool water or sport drinks before, during, and after a match.

- Use the shade on the court or at courtside during changeovers.

- Keep ice or an ice pack at courtside and use it on your neck, under your arms, and on the backs of your knees.

- Wear an air-vented hat.

- Use water-based sunscreen and reapply it often.

COLD

Playing in cold weather is not as bad as it might seem. The body has a remarkable capacity to warm up quickly. Once you get into the flow of a match or practice session, the cold temperature is not really a serious factor. Cold weather combined with strong winds is another story. Here are some suggestions to help you adjust to cold-weather conditions:

- Dress in layers and shed or add clothes as the exercise or weather intensity increases.

- Take as much time as allowed to warm up and get used to the cold weather.

- Don't take the full 90 seconds on changeovers unless you need it.

- Use a cut-out sock or glove on your dominant hand to keep it warm.

- Use heat packs designed to keep your hands warm.

- Wear a hat or cap to prevent heat loss.

- Drink fluids (warm, if desired) to stay hydrated.

Noise

Noise is a problem only if you are not used to it. If people are making enough noise to warrant a complaint, either tolerate it or ask them to be quiet. If the noise is coming from traffic, from construction work being done near the courts, or from passersby, learn to live with the noise or choose a quieter place to play, if possible.

Actually, once you learn to play with a lot of noise, your concentration should improve. If you can concentrate in noisy areas, you should be able to concentrate even better in quiet surroundings. Players who learn to play on noisy public courts probably have an advantage over club players used to quieter surroundings. Dealing with distractions, whether it's the other player or playing conditions, is a challenge of concentration, not tennis skills.

SUCCESS SUMMARY

Skills for this step are more mental than physical, and simulating game situations is not easy. The following scoring summary lists the drills that tested your ability to manage difficult situations. Enter your score for each drill and total your points. A score of 40 or more points out of 80 is a good one.

Becoming a successful tennis player involves a lot more than just hitting the ball over the net. Playing against different players in all types of situations makes the sport even more fun and challenging. A variety of distractions can level the playing field by allowing players with certain strengths to take advantage of them. Variety also makes it possible for weaker players to devise game plans that make them more competitive against superior opponents. When you reach a point in your tennis life at which you no longer worry about stroke technique and are able to focus instead on more sophisticated elements of the game, you know you're making progress.

SCORING SUMMARY

SPECIAL SITUATION DRILLS

Concentration Drills

1. Silent practice   _____ out of 10

2. Deuce games   _____ out of 10

3. Five goals   _____ out of 10

Adjusting to Opponents Drills

4. Take your best shot   _____ out of 10

5. Plan a point   _____ out of 10

6. 0-40 games   _____ out of 10

7. Handicap scoring   _____ out of 10

8. One free cheat   _____ out of 10

Total   _____ **out of 80**

The title of this book is *Tennis: Steps to Success*. The word *steps* is there for a reason. The idea is to build one stroke on top of another until you have a complete game—or at least a game as complete as it can be while under construction. Don't wait for perfection. The greatest players in the world are not perfect. They wrestle with the same problems that you will encounter on groundstrokes, serves, net play, and distractions in the mental game. Along the way, you can add the extras of specialty shots, tactics, strategy, and how to handle all of the outside elements that go with the sport of tennis. With a little talent, a lot of effort, and some luck, you might be able to take your steps to success a little faster than others. Whether you go fast or slow, enjoy the journey.

Preventing Tennis Injuries

Warming up for a tennis lesson, class, or match is important not only for preventing injuries but also for improving performance. Cooling down properly and safely gets your body back to normal and may help prepare you for the next time you play. In between, tennis players can sustain injuries. In this section, you'll read about current guidelines for warming up and cooling down as well as common tennis injuries, their treatment, and their prevention.

WARMING UP

Regardless of the sport, exercise physiologists agree that the first stage of warming up before play should involve an activity that increases the heart rate and blood circulation, raises the body's core temperature, and results in a light sweat. The first phase varies from person to person. Easing joint stiffness with a warm shower before going to the courts works for some. Warm, moist towels or wraps and warm-up apparel (a jacket or windbreaker) increase body temperature. But the most practical first-stage warm-up method without extra equipment is light jogging.

Jog around the courts or combine jogging toward the net, sidestepping away from the net, and shuffle-stepping (one foot does not cross in front of the other) to move laterally across the court while facing the net. Figure 1 shows an example of a warm-up jog routine.

Perhaps the most dramatic change in warm-ups in recent years involves the concept of stretching. The second phase of a warm-up in the past included static stretching—upper- or lower-body stretches that are held for 20 to 30 seconds and then

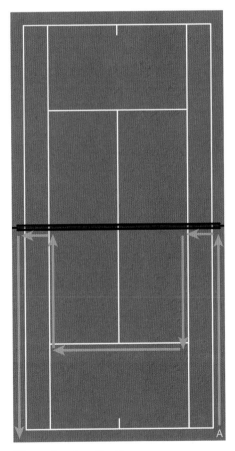

Figure 1   Jog the lines.

repeated several times. Static stretches are no longer recommended because the evidence shows that sustained stretching can cause muscles to become less explosive and diminish athletic performance. Save static stretches for the cool-down after a match or practice session.

Foam rollers are used to loosen muscle tissue and literally to work the knots out. They are inexpensive and an effective replacement for static stretching as the second phase of a warm-up. The person moves upper- or lower-body muscle groups forward and backward against the roller, using the weight of the body to create pressure. Think of it as self-massage, or the medical term, myofascial release. However, foam rollers are not practical for use on a tennis court surface, and most tennis players simply won't use them unless they do so at home or in a locker room.

The third warm-up phase is ballistic stretching. The term *ballistic* refers to using the motions you'll use while playing tennis, but beginning slowly, with gradual increases until you are moving and swinging as you would in a match.

Tennis players like phase 3 because that's what they've been doing as a warm-up (minus the jogging) since the sport was invented. A few hundred years later, scientists have discovered that hitting forehands, backhands, volleys, lobs, smashes, and serves is a good way to warm up for a tennis match.

If your practice partner is willing to cooperate, start just behind the service line in the middle of the court and exchange soft, short groundstrokes. Next, move to the baseline and hit controlled forehands and backhands. Alternate roles with your partner to practice down-the-line and crosscourt groundstrokes. Then take turns while one player volleys and the other hits groundstrokes. Finally, set up your practice partner so that she can hit a few controlled smashes from your lobs; then reverse roles again while you hit the smashes. Before a match begins, hit practice serves from the deuce and ad courts.

Following is a step-by-step review of phase 3 of a typical tennis warm-up before a competitive match (note that an opponent in a real match may or may not want to warm up with the same shots or the same sequence of shots):

- Jogging lines (before opponent arrives)
- Groundstroke exchanges (both players back)
- Volley versus groundstroke exchanges (one up, one back; reverse roles)
- Lob versus controlled smash exchanges (one up, one back; reverse roles)
- Service exchanges (deuce and ad courts; some players return serves, but most allow the other player to serve two or three balls in a row before serving them back)

COOLING DOWN

After a match or practice session, don't just finish the last point, walk off the court, and get in a car to go home. Take a few minutes to cool down. It reduces the risk of blood pooling in your legs, avoids the risk of a sudden drop in blood pressure, and allows your pulse rate to begin returning to normal in a controlled manner. One suggestion is to cool down until your pulse rate drops below 100 beats per minute. Your level of fitness is improving if your recovery time is declining.

If you've been hitting during a practice session, take a few minutes to pick up the balls, or walk around the perimeter of the doubles court for five minutes. Put a warm-up suit on (or at least a jacket) for a few minutes, even if the weather is hot. Try to minimize abrupt changes in your body temperature.

Next, take a few minutes to go through some static stretches—the same kind you used in the past before matches. There is evidence that static stretching increases subsequent range of motion. Include stretches for the upper body, trunk, and legs.

INJURIES

Tennis elbow gets most of the publicity, but several less serious, more common injuries occur among tennis players of all ages and abilities. Blisters, cramps, shin splints, sprains, and strains are problems all players encounter sooner or later (see table 1). Tennis injuries are not usually emergencies, and players who are well informed can take care of them without medical assistance.

Blisters

For tennis players, the two most likely places for blisters to develop are the racket hand (hand and racket friction) and the feet (shoe, sock, and foot friction). Shoes that don't fit properly, differences in court surfaces, heat, sweating, and an increased level of activity are all factors that could lead to the formation of blisters.

Part of the problem is that tennis players seldom stop playing when blisters begin to form, which results in a more severe problem. The early warning signs are red hot spots in the area affected and a stinging or burning sensation. Eventually, the skin area becomes white and swells with fluid, but it may or may not break.

Most blisters heal by themselves when the source of the friction is removed. If the top layer of skin stays intact, a doughnut-like pad placed over the top protects the skin and relieves the discomfort. The fluid can be drained if you have access to a sterile needle, but the overlying skin should be left as a protective dressing. If the skin has already been removed, treat the blistered area as you would an abrasion. Clean and rinse it with mild, soapy water or an antiseptic; then bandage it. Ask about over-the-counter medicated blister dressings at a pharmacy.

The best way to prevent a blister is to be aware of vulnerable areas and hot spots, and to take action to keep them from developing into blisters. Wearing a glove might protect the hand. Choosing shoes and socks that don't irritate the skin might save the feet. Shop for socks that maintain their cushioning properties and wick moisture away from the skin. Apply creams to areas subject to chafing.

Muscle Cramps

Not enough is known about why cramps—those sudden, involuntary, and painful muscle contractions—occur, and the reasons might vary from person to person. However, cramps are common among tennis players. Contributing factors appear to be hot and humid weather, intense exercise, sweating, fatigue, dehydration, and possible deficiencies in minerals such as calcium, sodium, potassium, and magnesium. If any of these minerals are depleted, muscles may not contract properly.

The perfect storm for a cramp would be a tennis player competing in a late spring or summer tournament (perhaps the first of the season) in a long, difficult match with tired muscles. By the time all of those factors come together, it may be too late to prevent a cramp.

Table 1   Injuries

Injury	Causes	Treatment
Blisters	• Hand and racket irritation • Foot, sock, and shoe irritation	• Keep surface area intact • If skin is torn, clean area • Apply liquid or doughnut bandage and tape
Muscle cramps	• Fatigue • Prolonged overexertion • Electrolyte depletion • Dehydration (even 1%)	• Stretch affected muscle • Ice • Pressure • Massage • Ingest fluids (water)
Shin splints	• Hard surfaces • Improper conditioning • Improper arch support • Poor shoe cushioning	• Rest (a few days) • Ice first, heat later (three or four days) • Compression • Elevation • Shoe inserts • Over-the-counter pain or anti-inflammatory medication
Sprains	• Joint forced beyond normal range of motion	• Protection • Rest • Ice first, heat later (three or four days) • Compression • Elevation • Stabilization • Over-the-counter pain or anti-inflammatory medication
Strains	• Overexertion • Overuse • Improper warm-up • Sudden movement • Fatigue	• Protection • Rest • Moderate compression • Ice • Elevation • Over-the-counter pain or anti-inflammatory medication
Tennis elbow	• Forearm stress • Improper hitting technique • Age combined with other factors • Overuse • Lack of strength or flexibility	• Rest • Ice first, heat later • Over-the-counter pain or anti-inflammatory medication • Elbow support, sleeve • Stretch muscles that extend wrist

More than 90 percent of cramps involve the quadriceps, hamstrings, or calves, and a cramp can affect a single muscle or an entire muscle group. The symptoms are unmistakable: visible, palpable, involuntary, violent muscle spasms and sharp, severe pain that lasts until the activity is stopped and the muscle in stretched, pressured, or massaged.

A common scenario is for a player to return to action immediately after a cramp subsides. When this happens, the muscle is likely to cramp again. The area may be sore for several days afterward. If the cramp persists, apply cold packs for 15 to 20 minutes three or four times a day.

Preventing cramps is a moving target, but diet, hydration, conditioning, daily routines, rest periods, and acclimatization are all factors that should be taken into consideration by players, teachers, coaches, and parents. Although it won't be always be practical, try to give yourself as many days as possible to get used to the environment in which you will train or compete.

One of the most reliable predictors of cramps is a history of previous cramping. Soft-tissue massage (with a foam roller) of the muscles prone to cramping, gentle stretching, and drinking plenty of fluids before, during, and after intense exercise might help you avoid the problem.

There is good news. Most cramps are not long-term, recurring conditions, and most of them subside within a few minutes, even though it may seem longer.

Shin Splints

Any athlete who pounds a hard surface repeatedly or puts unusual, added stress on the bones, muscles, and joints of the lower legs is vulnerable to shin splints. That puts beginners, advanced beginners, and intermediate tennis players in a high-risk group.

The condition is medically termed medial tibial stress syndrome, or tibial pain syndrome, but by any name, it refers to pain in the front or inner part of the lower leg. The pain is caused by irritation and inflammation. In addition to playing or practicing on hard, unfamiliar surfaces, shin splints can be caused by wearing old shoes that don't absorb shock; a sudden increase in training frequency, duration, or intensity; flat feet; or a previous history of shin splints.

Symptoms of shin splints come on gradually. They include lower-leg pain, pain when the toes or foot are bent downward, mild swelling in some cases, and tenderness along the front or inner part of the lower leg. In the early stages of shin splints, the pain is likely to subside when the person is not playing or practicing. Later, the pain is continuous.

Although the pain may be severe enough to keep you off the courts for a while, shin splints may respond to ice applications, rest, over-the-counter pain medications, compression sleeves, arch supports (if flat feet are the problem), or changing to shoes that provide more support and cushioning.

Preventing shin splints is preferable to treating them. There is usually an identifiable reason for the condition. Change tennis shoes before they lose their arch support and cushioning features, consider over-the-counter shoe inserts that prevent the ankle from rolling inward, and never dramatically increase training intensity or duration. Cross-training in another sport or activity such as walking, bicycling, or swimming might help you avoid shin splints. If you jog before practice to warm up or after practice to cool down, do it on grass rather than on a hard surface.

Sprains

A sprain occurs when a joint has been forced beyond its normal range of motion. One or more of the ligaments that hold the bones of that joint together have been overstretched, partially torn, or ruptured.

Ankle sprains are among the most common tennis injuries. One of the three ligaments that wraps around the outside of the ankle (the anterior talofibular ligament) is especially vulnerable and frequently injured. Up to 80 percent of all ankle sprains occur when the foot rolls toward the outside of the ankle. Basketball players have the highest incidence of ankle sprains. Sprains are also among the most common injuries sustained by tennis players.

Ankle sprains are classified according to the degree of tissue damage. Grade 1 sprains cause mild pain, localized swelling, and tenderness, but the ankle remains stable and is not bruised. The person can walk, but may not be able to jump or jog. The ligament has been overstretched but not torn, and slight, sometimes reparable damage to the ligament fibers has occurred.

Athletes who suffer a grade 2 ankle sprain may hear a popping or tearing sound when the ankle rolls to the side. There is significant bruising and internal bleeding, which might be observed three to four days after the injury. Tenderness, swelling, limited range of motion, and difficulty walking are other symptoms. The ligament has been partially torn, and the ankle is unstable.

In grade 3 sprains, the pain is extreme. Along with swelling and tenderness, there is major instability, great difficulty in walking, and a feeling that the ankle may give way. The ligament has been considerably or completely torn.

Depending on the severity of the sprain, initial treatment should include rest (24 to 48 hours), ice (15 to 20 minutes three or four times a day, with two hours between cold packs for one to three days), compression (with an elastic bandage), protection (with an air brace or ankle support), and elevation (propping up the leg and ankle level with the heart two to three hours a day). Over-the-counter pain relievers reduce pain; aspirin and ibuprofen reduce pain and address inflammation.

Develop strength and flexibility in the structures that make up the ankle joint. Flexibility of the Achilles tendon is especially important to withstand the forces placed on the ankle joint in tennis training and competition. Court shoes that provide lateral support will also help.

Strains

Strains—stretched or torn muscles or tendons—are informally called pulled muscles. Whereas sprains are more common in the ankles and knees of tennis players, strains can occur all over the body—in the fingers, hand, or wrist; the elbow, arm, or shoulder; the neck; the abdominal area; the back; the hip; the quads or hamstrings; the knee; or the ankle, foot, or toes—just about any area that houses a muscle–tendon unit. Muscles that lack flexibility or strength are especially vulnerable to strains.

Strains are injuries caused by any of the following:

- Overexertion (playing or practicing tennis too much or playing before completing an appropriate recovery period)

- Not warming up properly

- Sudden movements (moving quickly to cover the court)

- Fatigue (playing or practicing for long periods)

- Nutritional deficiencies

Like sprains, strains are classified according to the amount of damage. Grade 1 strains indicate a stretched muscle–tendon unit. In grade 2, a partial tear has occurred, and in grade 3, the unit is completely torn. Strains of the shoulder girdle can be a contributing factor to shoulder tendinitis.

If you suffer a strain, follow the same self-treatment guidelines as with sprains: protection, rest (for at least a day), ice, compression (but not too tight), and elevation. Over-the-counter medications ease the discomfort. If there is significant swelling, pain, fever, bleeding, or an inability to move or walk, seek immediate medical attention.

Once you begin hitting or playing again following a strain, take it easy. Gradually work back into playing condition. Heat applications before physical activity (a warm shower or warm, moist compresses) will increase circulation and loosen muscle tissues. Ice (packs, but not in direct contact with the skin) afterward will control swelling and reduce pain.

Preventing strained, or pulled, muscles requires strong and flexible muscles and a well-executed warm-up before exercising or playing tennis.

Tennis Elbow

Tennis elbow, medically termed epicondylitis, results from repetitive stress, overuse, and muscle strain injury that affect the forearm muscles and tendons near the inside or outside of the elbow. It has always been one of the most common and difficult-to-heal sport injuries. Tennis elbow affects as many as half of all frequent tennis players, but it can be just as debilitating to golfers, baseball players, volleyball players, and others who may never play tennis. Anyone who regularly lifts, reaches, pushes, or pulls can sustain the injury. Also, a sudden impact, such as hitting the elbow against the corner of a countertop, can initiate a long-term problem.

Although repetitive contraction of the forearm muscles is thought to be the most common cause of tennis elbow, the exact cause may vary from person to person. When overuse is combined with factors such as age (over 35), frequency of play (three or more times a week), lack of strength or flexibility, off-center hitting, vibration-causing contact between the ball and racket strings, or holding the racket too tightly, the risk of tennis elbow increases. Any combination of those factors added to the repetitive contraction of forearm muscles can result in inflammation and, in some cases, degeneration of muscle and tendon tissue.

Most of the symptoms of tennis elbow involve pain and develop gradually. Among the possible signs are sharp pain on the inside or outside of the elbow, pain that radiates down the forearm, pain when the wrist is extended (bent upward), pain when shaking hands, pain when lifting objects (as light as a glass of water or a cup of coffee), tenderness, or a loss of grip strength.

The first step in treatment is to avoid the activity that causes the pain. Don't play tennis for a week or longer. Use ice applications and massage the area with ice for the first two or three days after symptoms appear. After 72 hours, moist heat may help, as will pain medications such as aspirin or ibuprofen taken according to directions. In the long term, elbow braces or wraps can redirect pressure away from the inflamed elbow.

Severe lateral epicondylitis won't go away by itself. If self-treatment is not producing results, see a sports medicine physician and inquire about more aggressive treatment options.

You might be able to prevent tennis elbow by working with a teaching professional to make sure you are using correct hitting technique. Consider using a two-handed backhand if tennis elbow symptoms occur when you use a one-handed grip. Try a racket that is slightly more or less flexible in the shaft, string tension with a deviation of 3 to 5 pounds (1.4 to 2.3 kg), and a grip that is soft enough to provide a cushioning effect. Exercises that extend the wrist will improve flexibility and arm strength.

Resources

To become more involved in the sport of tennis, consider joining the United States Tennis Association (USTA) or the national tennis organization for the country in which you live.

The USTA is the nonprofit governing body of tennis in the United States. Its mission is to promote and develop the growth of tennis. The USTA has 17 sections, some of which are divided into state associations. USTA income is derived from membership fees, product sales, and sponsorship of the U.S. Open, played each year at the USTA Billie Jean King National Tennis Center in New York. USTA members can play in tournaments and leagues, receive publications, get professional instruction, and obtain other benefits of belonging to an organization with hundreds of thousands of members.

Following is contact information for USTA sections, selected national tennis organizations, and international organizations.

USTA SECTIONS

USTA Caribbean: www.caribbean.usta.com

USTA Eastern: www.eastern.usta.com

USTA Florida: www.florida.usta.com

USTA Hawaii: www.hawaii.usta.com

USTA Intermountain: www.intermountain.usta.com

USTA Mid-Atlantic: www.midatlantic.usta.com

USTA Middle States: www.middlestates.usta.com

USTA Midwest: www.midwest.usta.com

USTA Missouri Valley: www.missourivalley.usta.com

USTA New England: www.newengland.usta.com

USTA Northern: www.northern.usta.com

USTA Northern California: www.norcal.usta.com

USTA Pacific Northwest: www.pnw.usta.com

USTA Southern: www.southern.usta.com

USTA Southern California: www.scta.usta.com

USTA Southwest: www.southwest.usta.com

USTA Texas: www.texas.usta.com

NATIONAL TENNIS ORGANIZATIONS

Australia: www.tennis.com.au

Canada: www.tenniscanada.com

China: www.tennis.org.cn

Colombia: www.fedecoltenis.com

France: www.fft.fr

Germany: www.dtb-tennis.de

Great Britain: www.lta.org.uk

India: www.aitatennis.com

Ireland: www.tennisireland.ie

Israel: www.ita.one.co.il

Italy: www.federtennis.it

Mexico: www.fmt.org.mx.

Netherlands: www.knltb.nl

New Zealand: www.tennisnz.com

Russia: www.tennis-russia.ru

Spain: www.rfet.es

South Africa: www.tennissa.co.za

INTERNATIONAL TENNIS ORGANIZATIONS

Asia: www.asiantennis.com

Europe: www.tenniseurope.org

United States: www.usta.com

International Tennis Federation: www.itftennis.com

Glossary

ace—A winning serve that the receiver cannot touch with the racket.

ad—Advantage; refers to the point after the score was deuce.

ad court—The left half of a player's court as the player faces the net from the baseline.

ad in—A reference to the score when the player serving has won the point after the score was deuce.

ad out—A reference to the score when the player receiving the serve has won the point after the score was deuce.

all—A tie score; 30 all, for example, means that the score is 30-30.

alley—A lane, 4 feet (1.2 m) wide, running the length of, and on both sides of, the singles court. The alleys are in play for all shots after the serve in doubles.

amateur—A person who does not accept money for playing or teaching tennis.

angle shot—A shot that crosses the net at a severe angle.

approach shot—A shot that the hitter follows to the net.

Association of Tennis Professionals (ATP)—An organization composed of most of the leading male players in the world.

Australian doubles—A doubles formation in which the player at the net (the server's partner) lines up on the same half of the doubles court as the server.

backcourt—The part of the court between the service line and the baseline.

backhand—A stroke that a right-handed player hits by reaching across the body to the left side; a left-handed player reaches across to the right side to hit a backhand.

backspin—Reverse spin on the ball, like a car wheel in reverse.

backswing—The preparation for a stroke in which the racket is drawn back before being swung forward.

balance point—The point of the racket shaft at which the head and the handle are balanced in weight.

baseline—The boundary line that runs parallel to, and 39 feet (11.9 m) from, the net.

block—The return of a ball with a very short, or no, swinging motion.

break point—The point on which one player can break the serve of an opponent.

carry—A shot that is carried on the racket strings, slung, or hit twice as the ball is returned. Carries are legal unless the player makes two or more deliberate attempts to hit the ball over the net; carries may be called by the umpire or the player who hits the ball.

center mark—A line, 2 inches (5 cm) wide and 14 inches (35.6 cm) long, dividing the baseline at the center. The server may not legally step on or past the center mark before striking the ball.

center service line—The line in the middle of the court, perpendicular to the net, that divides the two service courts.

center strap—A 3-foot (1 m) strap in the center of the net that is anchored to the surface of the court. The strap secures the net during play.

changeover—The 90-second break that players are allowed when changing ends of the court, when the total number of games played is an odd number.

chip—A groundstroke hit with a short backswing and with backspin on the ball. The chip is usually meant to be a shallow shot (not very deep into the opponent's court).

choke—To play poorly because of pressure of competition.

choke up—To hold the racket at a point higher on the handle, away from the base of the grip.

chop—A shot hit with backspin to any part of the court.

circuit—A series of tournaments at the state, sectional, national, or international level.

closed stance—A hitting position in which the foot closer to the net steps across the body toward the singles sideline instead of toward the net.

closed tournament—An event open only to players in a particular geographical area.

Coman tiebreaker—A tiebreak procedure that is identical to the regular tiebreaker except that the players change ends after the first point and then after every 4 points, and at the conclusion of the tiebreaker.

composite—A reference to tennis rackets made from the combination of two or more materials.

Continental (hammer) grip—Holding the racket so that the player does not have to change grips between forehand and backhand strokes; the wrist is directly over the top of the grip.

cross strings—Strings running horizontally from one side of the racket head to the other.

crosscourt—A shot hit diagonally from one corner of the court to the opposite corner.

Davis Cup—An international team tennis event for men.

deep—A reference to the area near the baseline.

default—The awarding of a match to one player or team because an opponent fails to appear or is not able to complete a match; synonym for *forfeit*.

deuce—A tie score at 40-40 and each tie thereafter in the same game.

deuce court—The right half of a player's court as the player faces the baseline.

dink—A shot hit with very little pace or depth.

double fault—Failure on both attempts to serve into the proper court.

doubles—A match played with four players.

down the line—A shot hit more or less parallel to the closer sideline.

draw—A method of determining who plays whom in a tournament.

drive—A groundstroke hit forcefully, low, and deeply into an opponent's court.

drop shot—A softly hit shot, usually having backspin, that barely clears the net.

drop volley—A drop shot hit with a volley.

Eastern backhand grip—A grip in which the V formed by the thumb and index finger is above but slightly toward the left of the racket as a right-handed player prepares to hit a backhand.

Eastern forehand grip—A grip in which the V formed by the thumb and index finger is above but slightly toward the right of the racket as a right-handed player prepares to hit a forehand.

electrolytes—Minerals such as calcium, sodium, potassium, and magnesium.

error—A point lost as a result of one player's unforced mistake.

face—The flat surface formed by the strings and the racket head.

fast—A description of a tennis court surface on which the ball skids and moves rapidly.

fault—Failure on an attempt to serve into the proper court.

Federation (Fed) Cup—An international team tennis event for women.

feed-in consolation—A tournament in which players who lose in the early rounds of a tournament reenter the championship draw and may finish as high as fifth place.

final—The match played to determine the winner of a tournament.

flat—A description of a shot hit with little or no spin. Also a term used to describe tennis balls that have lost their firmness and resilience.

flexibility—How much a racket bends from head to shaft or from one side of the head to the other at contact with the ball.

follow-through—The part of the swinging motion after the ball has been hit.

foot fault—Stepping onto the baseline or into the court before striking the ball when serving; this results in a service fault.

forcing shot—A shot hit with enough pace or depth to force an opponent into a difficult return.

forehand—A stroke that a right-handed player hits on the right side of the body and a left-handed player hits on the left side of the body.

forfeit—The awarding of a match to one player or team because an opponent has failed to appear or is not able to complete the match; synonym for *default*.

frame—The tennis racket, excluding the strings.

gauge—The measure of a string's thickness (the higher the number, the thinner the string).

graphite—A synthetic, carbon-based material 20 times stronger and stiffer than wood; often used in rackets.

grip—The manner in which a racket is held. Also, the part of the racket where it is held.

grommet—A small, round plastic sleeve in the frame through which the strings pass.

groove—To hit shots in a patterned, disciplined, and consistent manner.

groundstroke—A shot hit with a forehand or backhand stroke after the ball has bounced on the court.

gut—Racket string made from beef or sheep intestines.

hacker—A player who uses unorthodox techniques.

half volley—A shot hit just after the ball has bounced on the court; contact is made below knee level.

head—The upper part of the racket where the strings are attached.

head heavy—A racket that has a balance point more than 1/4 inch (6.35 mm) from the center (midpoint of the racket's length) toward the head.

head light—A racket that has a balance point more than 1/4 inch (6.35 mm) from the center (midpoint of the racket's length) toward the handle.

hindrance—A call made when a player is hindered by either an opponent or a spectator. It results in a let or a point awarded to the player hindered.

hitting surface—The stringed area of the racket head.

holding serve—A situation in which the server has won the game that he or she just served.

hook—A slang term meaning "to cheat."

inside-out backhand—Moving around the forehand to hit a backhand.

inside-out forehand—Moving around the backhand to hit a forehand.

International Tennis Federation (ITF)—The international governing body of tennis.

invitational tournament—A tournament open only to players who have been invited to participate.

junior racket—A racket less than 27 inches (68.6 cm) long that is usually lighter than standard rackets and has a smaller grip.

Kevlar—A synthetic fiber used to strengthen tennis racket frames.

ladder tournament—A competition in which the names of participants are placed in a column; players can advance up the column (ladder) by challenging and defeating players whose names appear above their own.

let—A serve that hits the top of the net and lands in the proper service court. Also, an expression used to indicate that a point should be replayed for any of a number of other reasons.

linesperson—An official who is responsible for calling shots either in or out at the baseline, service line, or center service line.

lob—A high-trajectory, arching shot.

lob volley—A lob hit with a volley.

long—An informal expression used to indicate that a shot went out past the baseline.

love—The term commonly used to say "zero" in the tennis scoring system.

main strings—The vertical strings, running from the top to the bottom of the racket head.

match—A competition between two players in singles, two pairs in doubles, or two teams, as when two school teams compete against each other.

match point—The stage of a match at which a player can win the match by winning the next point. The term is used by spectators and television announcers during a match and by players after a match. It is not, or should not be, used by the umpire or players in calling out the score.

mixed doubles—A competition pairing a man and woman on one team against a man and woman on the other team.

net game—Shots hit while playing near the net, such as volleys and smashes.

net tape—The strip of material attached to the top of the net.

net umpire—An official responsible for calling let serves.

no—An informal expression used by some players to call shots out.

no-ad scoring—A scoring system in which a maximum of 7 points constitutes a game. For example, if the score is tied at 3 points for each player, the next player to win a point wins the game.

no-man's land—The area of the court between the service line and the baseline. This area is usually considered a weak area from which to return shots during a rally.

nonsteroidal anti-inflammatory drugs (NSAIDs)—Prescription or over-the-counter medications used to reduce inflammation or pain.

not up—An expression used to indicate that a ball has bounced twice on the same side of the court before being hit.

nylon—A strong synthetic material commonly used for racket strings (rarely used by more experienced players).

off hand—The hand that does not hold the racket.

one-up, one-down wheelchair tennis—A doubles competition that pairs a wheelchair player with an able-bodied player.

open racket face—The position of the racket when the racket face is angled upward, away from the court surface.

open stance—A hitting position in which the feet are parallel to the net.

open tennis—Competitions open to amateur and professional players.

out—A call indicating that a shot has bounced outside a boundary line.

over-the-counter drugs (OTCs)—Medications used to reduce inflammation or pain that do not require a prescription.

overgrip—A one-piece grip that is wrapped over the original racket grip.

overhead smash—A hard, powerful stroke hit from an over-the-head racket position.

pace—The velocity with which a ball is hit, or the velocity of the ball.

passing shot—A groundstroke hit out of reach of an opponent at the net.

percentage shot—The safest, most effective shot hit in a particular situation.

percentage tennis—A style of playing that emphasizes hitting the most effective shot in every situation and reducing errors.

placement—Hitting a shot to an open area of the court.

playing pro—A person who makes a living playing tennis.

poaching—When a doubles player at the net cuts in front of the partner to hit a volley.

point penalty—A system in which players are penalized points, games, or even matches for improper conduct.

pro set—A match that is completed when one player or team has won at least eight games and is ahead by at least two games.

professional (pro)—A person who plays or teaches tennis for money.

pronation—A movement of the wrist in which it is turned down and away from the body on contact with the ball during a serve.

pusher—A type of player who is consistent but who hits with very little pace.

put-away—A shot that is literally put away (out of reach) from an opponent.

racket face—The hitting surface (strings) of a tennis racket.

rally—An exchange of shots hit back and forth.

range of motion (ROM)—The range of movement (flexion and extension) possible for a joint.

ready position—The position in which a player stands while waiting for a shot.

receiver—The player to whom a serve is hit.

referee—An official responsible for supervising all competition during a tournament, from making the draw to the last point played.

retrieving—Getting to and returning a difficult shot.

retriever—A player who gets every ball back but does not play aggressively.

round-robin—A competition in which all participants compete against each other in a series of matches. The player or team finishing the competition with the best win–loss percentage is the winner.

rush—To move toward the net following a forcing shot.

second—An informal expression used by some payers to remind the receiver that the second serve is being played after a slight interruption.

semifinals—Matches played to determine the finalists in a tournament.

semiopen stance—A hitting position between an open and square stance in which the feet are aligned so that the body is partially open to the net.

semi-Western forehand grip—A way of holding a racket that is approximately halfway between an Eastern and Western forehand grip.

serve—The shot used to put the ball into play at the beginning of a point.

server—The player who begins a point with a serve.

service break—The loss of a game by the player serving.

service court—Either of two alternating areas into which the ball must be served; its boundaries are the net, the center line, the service line, and the singles sidelines.

service line—The line that is parallel to, and 21 feet (6.4 m) from, the net.

set—The part of the match that is completed when a player or team has won at least six games and is ahead by at least two games.

set point—The stage of a set when a player or team can win the set by winning the next point.

shadow swing—Like shadow boxing, a practice method in which a player goes through the motions of a swing without hitting a ball.

shaft—The part of the racket between the head and the grip.

sideline—The boundary line that runs from the net to the baseline. The singles sidelines are closer to the center of the court than the doubles sidelines.

single-elimination tournament—A type of competition in which players who win their first match advance to the next round of competition, whereas those who lose a match are eliminated from competition.

slice—To hit the ball with sidespin, like the spin of a top.

slow—The description of a court surface on which the ball bounces and slows down after the bounce.

smash—See *overhead smash.*

split sets—An expression used to indicate that two players or teams have each won a set.

split step—A footwork technique in which the player briefly squares the feet when approaching the net just before hitting a volley.

square stance—A position in which the toes of both feet form a line parallel to either sideline.

straight sets—Winning a match without losing a set.

stroke—The manner in which a ball is hit (forehand, backhand, volley, and so on).

sweet spot—The exact place on the racket face that produces controlled power with no vibration (may also be referred to commercially as the *power zone*).

synthetic gut—A type of racket string made from specially designed nylon.

T—The location on a tennis court where the center service line intersects the service line to form the letter T.

take two—An expression meaning that the server should repeat the first service attempt, starting the point over.

tank—To deliberately lose a point or a match.

teaching pro—A person who is paid to teach people to play tennis.

tennis elbow—An injury to the forearm tendon that is attached to the outer part of the elbow.

throat—The part of the racket just below the head.

tiebreaker—A method of completing a set when both players or teams have won six games.

titanium—A strong, lustrous white metal used in small amounts in the construction of some rackets.

topspin—Bottom-to-top rotation on a ball, like a car wheel going forward.

touch—The ability to hit a variety of precision shots.

umpire—A person responsible for officiating a match between two players or teams.

unforced error—A point lost with no pressure having been exerted by the opponent.

United States Tennis Association (USTA)—A national, noncommercial membership organization whose mission is to promote and develop the game of tennis.

vibration dampener—A rubber or plastic device inserted at the base of the racket strings (near the throat) to reduce the vibration on impact with the ball.

volley—A shot hit before the ball bounces on the court.

Western grip—A way of holding the racket in which the wrist is positioned directly behind the handle.

wide—An expression used by some players to indicate a shot when out beyond the sideline.

wide body—A description of a racket frame with a very wide head.

Wimbledon—A tournament in England, generally considered to be the most prestigious in the world.

World Tennis Association (WTA)—An organization consisting of the world's leading female professional players.

yoke—The part of the racket immediately below the head; the upper part of the shaft; the throat.

About the Authors

Jim Brown, PhD, has taught, coached, played, and written about tennis for over 40 years. He is the executive editor of the *Steadman Philippon Research Institute News* and a regular contributor to health publications of the Cleveland Clinic, Duke School of Medicine, and the David Geffen School of Medicine at UCLA. He has served as the editor of *Tennis Industry* magazine, *Tennis Clinic*, *Georgia Tech Sports Medicine & Performance Newsletter*, and *Sports Performance Journal*.

Dr. Brown has written, coauthored, or edited 14 books and hundreds of articles on sports, sports medicine, health, and education. He has been published extensively online, having written columns for CBS Sportsline.com, USTA-Southern Section, CorePerformance.com, and WebMD. His work has appeared in such notable printed publications as *Sports Illustrated for Women*, *Washington Post*, *Better Homes and Gardens*, *Raising Teens*, and *New York Post*.

During Dr. Brown's teaching career, he served as a clinician for the United States Tennis Association; the American Alliance for Health, Physical Education, Recreation and Dance; and the President's Council on Physical Fitness and Sports.

He lives in Atlanta, Georgia.

Camille Soulier is a physical education instructor at Pearl River Community College and director of junior and adult tennis programs at the Kamper Park Tennis Complex in Hattiesburg, Mississippi. She has collaborated with Jim Brown on a variety of teaching, coaching, and writing projects and enjoyed a successful playing career at both the collegiate and USTA sectional and national levels.

She currently holds numerous positions in the United States Tennis Association. Most recently, she served as the head coach for the PRCC men's and women's tennis team, where she was named the Region 23 Coach of the Year in 2000.

Camille lives in Hattiesburg, Mississippi.